A NEW NOTION

Two Works by C.L.R. James

Every Cook Can Govern;
The Invading Socialist Society

Edited and with an introduction by
Noel Ignatiev

AAKAR

A NEW NOTION: TWO WORKS BY C.L.R. JAMES
Edited and with an introduction by Noel Ignatiev

Published in agreement with PM Press, Oakland, CA
for publication and sale only in the Indian Subcontinent
(India, Pakistan, Bangladesh, Nepal, Maldives,
Bhutan & Sri Lanka)

First Published in India, 2011

ISBN 978-93-5002-097-5 (Pb)

Published by
AAKAR BOOKS
28 E Pocket IV, Mayur Vihar Phase I, Delhi 110 091
Phone : 011 2279 5505 Telefax : 011 2279 5641
aakarbooks@gmail.com; www.aakarbooks.com

Printed at
Mudrak, 30 A, Patparganj, Delhi 110 091

Contents

The World View of C.L.R. James

NOEL IGNATIEV

Cyril Lionel Robert James was born in Trinidad in 1901 to a middle-class black family. He grew up playing cricket (which he credited with bringing him into contact with the common folk of the island). He also reported on cricket, and wrote a novel, several short stories, and a biography of Captain Cipriani, a Trinidadian labor leader and advocate of self-government. In 1932, James moved to England, where he covered cricket for the *Manchester Guardian* and became heavily involved in Marxist politics.

He wrote a history of the San Domingo revolution and a play based on that history, in which he and Paul Robeson appeared on the London stage. He wrote a history of the Communist International, *The History of Negro Revolt*, and translated into English Boris Souvarine's biography of Stalin. Together with his childhood friend, George Padmore, James founded the International African Service Bureau, which became a center for the struggle for the independence of Africa, helping to develop Jomo Kenyatta, Kwame Nkrumah, and others. He also spent time with coal miners in Wales (among whom he reported he felt no consciousness of race).

In 1938, James came to the United States on a speaking tour, ending up staying for fifteen years. He had discussions with Trotsky in Mexico and took part in the Trotskyist movement in the U.S. While in the U.S., James wrote a study of Hegel and the application of the dialectic in the modern world, a study of Herman Melville, a three-hundred-page outline for a study of American life (later published as *American Civilization*), and a number of shorter works (including the first of the two in this volume). During World War II he lived among and organized sharecroppers in southeastern Missouri. In 1952 James was arrested and interned on Ellis Island; the following year he was deported from the U.S. (His deportation was perhaps one of the greatest triumphs of McCarthyism: how might history have been different had he been in the country during Malcolm X's rise?)

For most of the next few years, C.L.R. James lived in the United Kingdom, returning to Trinidad briefly to edit *The Nation* (the paper of the People's National Movement) and serve as secretary of the Federal West Indian Labour Party (which advocated a West Indian federation). He left in 1961 after a falling out with Eric Williams, Prime Minister of Trinidad and a former student of James's, over Williams's turn toward supporting U.S. imperialism. Before leaving, he delivered a series of lectures aimed at providing the citizens of the new nation with a perspective on Western history and culture; these lectures, which for years were kept locked in a warehouse in Trinidad, have been published under the title, *Modern Politics*.

In 1968, taking advantage of the rising mood of revolution on the campuses, a group of black American students at Northwestern University brought James to the U.S. There he held university teaching posts and lectured widely until 1980. For the last years of his life, he lived in south London and lectured on politics, Shakespeare, and other topics. He died there in 1989.

In the West Indies, James is honored as one of the fathers of independence, and in Britain as a historic pioneer of the black movement; he is regarded generally as one of the major figures in Pan-Africanism. And he led in developing a current within Marxism that was democratic, revolutionary, and internationalist.

Obviously, this is a great variety of activities for a single individual to undertake. If the word "genius" has any meaning, then it must be applied to C.L.R. James. Most important, however, is not his individual qualities, but the worldview that enabled him to bring light to so many different spheres of activity. James says in *Notes on Organization* that when you develop a new notion, it is as if you have lifted yourself to a plateau from which you can look at familiar things from a new angle. What was James's *notion*, and how did it enable him to make unique contributions in so many areas?

For James, the starting point was that the working class is revolutionary. He did not mean that it is potentially revolutionary, or that it is revolutionary when imbued with correct ideas, or when led by the proper vanguard party. He said the working class is revolutionary and that its daily activities constitute the revolutionary process in modern society.

This was not a new idea. Karl Marx had said, first, that capitalism revolutionizes the forces of production and, second, that foremost among the forces of production is the working class. James, in rediscovering the idea and scraping off the rust that had accumulated over nearly a century, brought it into a modern context and developed it.

James's project was to discover, document, and elaborate the aspects of working-class activity that constitute the revolution in today's world. This project enabled James and his co-thinkers to look in a new way at the struggles of labor, black people, women, youth, and the colonial peoples, and to produce a body of literature far ahead of its time, works that still constitute indispensable guides for those fighting for a new world.

James and his co-thinkers focused their attention on the point of production, the scene of the most intense conflicts between capital and the working class. In two trailblazing works, "An American Worker" (1947) and "Punching Out" (1952), members of the Johnson-Forest Tendency led by James documented the emergence on the shop floor of social relations counter to those imposed by management and the union, relations that prefigured the new society.

Not every example James cited was from production. In "Negroes and American Democracy" (1956) he wrote, "the defense of their full citizenship rights by Negroes is creating a new concept of citizenship and community. When, for months, 50,000 Negroes in Montgomery, Alabama do not ride buses and overnight organize their own system of transportation, welfare, and political discussion and decision, that is the end of representative democracy. The community as the center of full and free association and as the bulwark of the people against the bureaucratic state, the right of women to choose their associates as freely as men, the ability of any man to do any job if given the opportunity, freedom of movement and of association as the expansion rather than the limitation of human personality, the American as a citizen not just of one country but of the world – all this is the New World into which the Negro struggle is giving everybody a glimpse..."

That is the new society and there is no other: ordinary people, organized around work and activities related to it, taking steps in opposition to capital to expand their freedom and their capacities as fully developed individuals. It is a leap of imagination, but it is the key to his method. Of course the new society does not triumph without an uprising; but it exists. It may be stifled temporarily; capital, after all, can shut down the plant, or even a whole industry, and can starve out an entire community. But the new society springs up elsewhere. If you want to know what the new society looks like, said James, study the daily activities of the working class.

James insisted that the struggles of the working class are the chief motor in transforming society. Even before it overthrows capital, the working class compels it to new stages in its development. Looking back at U.S. history, the resistance of the craftsmen compelled capital to develop methods of mass production; the workers responded to mass production by organizing the CIO, an attempt to impose their control on the rhythms of production; capital retaliated by incorporating the union into its administrative apparatus; the workers answered with the wildcat strike and a whole set of shop-floor relations outside of the union; capital responded to this autonomous activity by moving the industries out of the country in search of a more pliant working class and introducing computerized production to eliminate workers altogether. The working class has responded to the threat of permanent separation from the means of obtaining life with squatting, rebellion and food riots; this is a continuous process, and it moves the society forward – ending, as Marx said, in the revolutionary reconstitution of society at large, or in the common ruin of the contending classes.

James observed the triumph of the counter-revolution in Russia, the crushing of the workers' movement in Europe by fascism, and the role of the Communist Parties, and he concluded that these developments indicated that capitalism had reached a new stage. This new stage, like every development of capitalist society, was a product of workers' activity. The labor bureaucracy, that alien force ruling over the working class, grows out of the accomplishments of the workers' movement. In a modern society like the U.S., the working class struggles not against past defeats but against past victories – against the institutions that the workers themselves have created and which have become forms of domination over them. The social role of the labor bureaucracy is to absorb, and if necessary repress, the autonomous movement of the working class, and it scarcely matters whether it is Communist in France, Labour in Britain, or the AFL-CIO in this country.

"The Stalinist bureaucracy is the American bureaucracy carried to its ultimate and logical conclusion; both of them products of capitalist production in the epoch of state-capitalism," wrote James in *State Capitalism and World Revolution* (1950). In that work he called the new stage state capitalism, a system in which the state assumes the functions of capital and the workers remain exploited proletarians. He said that Russia was this type of society. Others before him had come to similar conclusions. James's theory was distinctive: it was a theory not of Russia but of the world. It applied to Germany, England, and the U.S. as much as to Russia. He wrote, "What the American workers are revolting against since 1936 and holding at bay, this, and nothing else but this, has overwhelmed the Russian proletariat. The rulers of Russia perform the same functions as are performed by Ford, General Motors, the coal operators and their huge bureaucratic staffs." This understanding of the "organic similarity of the American labour bureaucracy and the Stalinists" prepared James and his colleagues to see the Hungarian Revolution of 1956, the French General Strike of 1968, and the emergence of the U.S. wildcat strikes of the 1950s and the League of Revolutionary Black Workers in Detroit in 1967 as expressions of a global revolt against the domination of capital.

In an industrial country, it is not the guns and tanks of the government that hold the workers down. When the working class moves, the state is powerless against it. This was true in Hungary in 1956, it was true in France in 1968, and it was true in Poland in 1980. It is not guns and tanks but the relations of capital within the working class, the deals that different sectors of it make with capital, that hold the workers back. According to James, the working class develops through the overcoming of internal antagonisms, not external foes. He saw a civil war within the ranks of the working class and within the mind of each individual worker: two ways of looking at the world, not necessarily fully articulated, manifest in different sorts of behavior. Consistent with this notion, he saw the autonomous activities of groups within the working class as a crucial part of its self-development. As a Marxist, James believed that the working class, "united, disciplined, and organized by the very mechanism of capitalist production," had a special role to play in carrying the revolution through to the end. But he also believed that the struggles of other groups had their own validity, and that they represented challenges to the working people as a whole to build a society free of the domination of one class over another. In "The Revolutionary Answer to the Negro Problem in the U.S.A." (1948), he opposed "any attempt to subordinate or push to the rear the social and political significance of the independent Negro struggle for democratic rights." In that same work, written long before the Black Power movement, James spoke of the need for a mass movement responsible only to the black people, outside of the control of any of the Left parties.

He and his colleagues adopted a similar attitude toward the struggles of women and youth. "A Woman's Place" (1950), produced by members of the tendency led by James, examined the daily life of working-class woman, in the home, the neighborhood, and the factory, and took an unequivocal stand on the side of women's autonomy. They brought the same insights to the struggle of youth.

James also paid close attention to the struggle against colonialism. In 1938, he wrote *The Black Jacobins: Toussaint L'Ouverture and the San Domingo Revolution.* In that work he spoke of the tremendous creative force of the colonized peoples of Africa and the West Indies, and established the link between the masses of San Domingo and the masses of Paris.

His appreciation of the struggles of black people, of women, of youth, of the colonial peoples expressed his dialectical thinking. Here you have this revolutionary working class, said James, and at the same time you have the domination of capital, which also expresses itself within the working class. One of the places this conflict appeared was in culture.

The dominant tradition among Marxists held that popular culture is just brainwashing, a distraction from the class struggle. To James and his co-thinkers, the point was: how do the outlines of the new world manifest themselves in culture? In *Mariners, Renegades and Castaways: The Story of Herman Melville and the World We Live In* (1953), James demonstrated that the struggle for the new society was a struggle between different philosophies as they are lived. (It is my personal favorite among his works; among other virtues, it offers the most exciting explanation I have ever read of the process of literary creation.) His autobiographical book on cricket, *Beyond a Boundary* (1962), was not merely a sports book. It was about the people he knew intimately in the West Indies, and how their actions on the playing field showed the kind of people they were. There is a need for a similar study of basketball and the Afro-American people. Anybody can write about how black athletes are exploited by the colleges and later on by professional basketball and the TV and the shoe manufacturers – and all that is true. But for James the question was, How have the black people placed their stamp on the game and used it to express their vision of a new world?

Consider the figure of Michael Jordan in this light. Here is a person who has achieved self-powered flight. Every time he goes up with the ball, he is saying *in your face* to the society of exploitation and repression. His achievements are not his alone, but the product of an entire community with a history of struggle and resistance. The contrast between the general position of the Afro-American people, pinned to the ground, and the flight they have achieved on the basketball court is an example of the new society within the shell of the old. (I wrote this paragraph in 1992; since then, a book has appeared that does for basketball what James did for cricket: *Hoop Roots* by John Edgar Wideman. Wideman has said he wrote it with a copy of *Beyond a Boundary* on his desk.)

The task of freeing that new society from what inhibits it led James to a certain concept of organization. It has been asserted that James opposed organization – more particularly, that he opposed any form of organization that assigned distinctive tasks to those who sought to dedicate their lives to making revolution. The general charge is easily refuted: James spent his whole life building organizations of one kind or another, from the International African Service Bureau in Britain to a sharecroppers' union in Missouri to the Workers and Farmers Party in Trinidad. The function of these organizations was not to "lead the working class" but to accomplish this or that specific task. The more particular charge requires closer examination.

James argued that, in industrial societies, in which the very mechanism of capitalist production unites, disciplines, and organizes the working class, in which people take for granted modern communications and mass movements, the idea that any self-perpetuating group of people can set itself up to lead the working class is reactionary and bankrupt. In other words, he was a determined opponent of the vanguard party idea. But he did more than curse the Stalinists (and Trotskyites, whom he called "the comedians of the vanguard party"): in *Notes on Dialectics: Hegel, Marx, Lenin* (1948), he analyzed the organizational history of the workers' movement, and showed that the vanguard party reflected a certain stage of its development.

In that same work, James anticipated the new mass movements (France, Poland) that would erase the distinction between party and class. (He did not oppose the vanguard party for peasant countries, where he thought something like it might be necessary to mobilize and direct the mass movement – but even there he searched for ways to expand the area of autonomous activity. *Nkrumah and the Ghana Revolution*, a collection of articles and letters he wrote between 1958 and 1970, shows James grappling with the problem of leadership in a country where the forces of production are undeveloped. It is the least satisfying of his works.)

In modern society, whoever leads the working class keeps it subordinated to capital. A revolutionary crisis is defined precisely by the breakdown of the traditional institutions and leadership of the working class. James argued that it was among the sectors of society least touched by official institutions that relations characteristic of the new society would first appear. It is not the job of the conscious revolutionaries to "organize" the mass movements; that is the job of union functionaries and other bureaucrats.

James's rejection of the vanguard party, however, did not lead him to reject Marxist organization. For proof, one need only recall the great attention and energy he dedicated to building Facing Reality, an avowedly Marxist organization headquartered in Detroit with branches around the U.S. (These efforts are recounted and documented in *Marxism for Our Times: C.L.R. James on Revolutionary Organization*, edited by Martin Glaberman.) But what would the Marxist organization do? This is where it gets difficult. I once asked him that question and got from him the reply, "Its job is not to lead the workers." Very well, I said, but what was it to *do*? For an answer, I got the same: It was not to act like a vanguard party. It was obvious that James was not going to elaborate with me, a person who might for all he knew carry with him the vanguardist prejudices of the "left" he had been fighting for decades. I would have to extrapolate the answer from his works. To these, then, I turned.

In *Facing Reality*, coauthored by James, Grace Boggs and Cornelius Castoriadis, in the section "What To Do and How to Do It," it says, "Its task is to recognize and record." That is a start. Over the next few pages, *Facing Reality* lays out a plan for a popular paper that will document the new society as it emerges within the shell of the old. As should surprise no one, it is most concrete when discussing what was then called "The Negro Question in the United States":

> For the purpose of illustrating the lines along which the paper of the Marxist organization has to face its tasks (that is all we can do), we select two important issues, confined to relations among white and Negro workers, the largest sections of the population affected.
>
> 1) Many white workers who collaborate in the most democratic fashion in the plants continue to show strong prejudice against association with Negroes outside the plant.
>
> 2) Many Negroes make race relations a test of all other relations...
>
> What, then, is the paper of the Marxist organization to do?...
>
> Inside such a paper Negro aggressiveness takes its proper place as one of the forces helping to create the new society. If a white worker... finds that articles or letters expressing Negro aggressiveness on racial questions makes the whole paper offensive

to him, that means it is he who is putting his prejudices on the race question before the interests of the class as a whole. He must be reasoned with, argued with, and if necessary fought to a finish.

How is he to be reasoned with, argued with, and if necessary fought to a finish? First by making it clear that his ideas, his reasons, his fears, his prejudices also have every right in the paper....

The paper should actively campaign for Negroes in the South to struggle for their right to vote and actually to vote.... If Negroes outside of the South vote, now for the Democratic Party and now for the Republican, they have excellent reasons for doing so, and their general activity shows that large numbers of them see voting and the struggle for Supreme Court decisions merely as one aspect of a totality. They have no illusions. The Marxist organization retains and expresses its own view. But it understands that it is far more important, within the context of its own political principles, of which the paper is an expression, within the context of its own publications, meetings, and other activities in its own name, within the context of its translations and publications of the great revolutionary classics and other literature, that the Negroes make public their own attitudes and reasons for their vote. [*Published 1958; given the massive disenfranchisement of black people in 2000, 2004* and *2008, which no major or minor candidate has chosen to make an issue, it might not be a bad thing if revolutionaries, without abandoning their view of the electoral system, were to join in a campaign on behalf of prisoners' right to vote – NI.*]

Such in general is the function of the paper of a Marxist organization in the United States on the Negro question. It will educate, and it will educate above all white workers in their understanding of the Negro question and into a realization of their own responsibility in ridding American society of the cancer of racial discrimination and racial consciousness. The Marxist organization will have to fight for its own position, but its position will not be the wearisome repetition of "Black and White, Unite and Fight." It will be a resolute determination to bring all aspects of the question into the open, within the context of the recognition that the new society exists and that it carries within itself much of the sores and diseases of the old.

While the above passage focuses on the role of a paper, it provides a guide for other aspects of work. James's approach was in the best tradition of Lenin (whom James much admired). Lenin, it must be remembered, did not invent the soviets (councils). What he did, that no one else at the time was able to do, not even the workers who invented them, was to recognize in the soviets the political form of the new society. The slogan he propagated, "All Power to the Soviets," represented the intervention of the Marxist intellectual in the revolutionary process. In basing his policy on the soviets, those "spontaneous" creations of the Russian workers, he was far removed from what has come to be understood as vanguardism.

I recall once in the factory, a group of workers walking out in response to a plant temperature of one-hundred degrees-plus with no fans. Our little group, schooled in the teachings of James and Lenin, understanding that the walkout represented a way of dealing with grievances outside of the whole management-union contract system, agitated for a meeting to discuss how to make that walkout the starting point of a new shop-floor organization based on direct action. That was not vanguardism but critical intervention.

Another example from personal experience: I once worked a midnight shift in a metalworking plant. There were two other workers in the department on that shift, Jimmy and Maurice. Maurice had been having money troubles, which caused him to drink more than he should, which led to missed days and more trouble on the job, which led to troubles at home, etc. I came to work one night after missing the previous night, and Jimmy told me that Maurice had brought a pistol to the plant the night before, planning to shoot the general foreman if he reprimanded him in the morning about his attendance. "Did you try to stop him?" I asked. "No, what for?" queried Jimmy. "What happened?" I responded. "When the foreman came in," explained Jimmy, "instead of stopping to hassle Maurice, he just said hello and kept going to his office. He doesn't know how close he came to dying."

I, of course, did not want Maurice to shoot the general foreman because I did not want him to spend the rest of his life in prison for blowing away an individual who was no worse than the generality of his type. Jimmy looked at matters differently: for him, Maurice's life was already a prison that could be salvaged by one dramatic NO, regardless of the consequences. Who was right? Well, I had read all the books and knew that ninety-nine times out of a hundred nothing would come of Maurice's action: the plant guards or the cops would take him away or kill him on the spot. But on the hundredth time, something different might happen: the workers would block the plant guards, fight the cops, and the next thing you knew you had the mutiny on the Potemkin. The new society is the product of those two kinds of knowledge, Jimmy's and mine, and neither could substitute for the other. As a person who had decided to devote his life to revolution, my job was to Recognize and Record the new society as it made its appearance.

In 1969, a black worker at a Los Angeles aircraft plant, Isaac ("Ike") Jernigan, who had been harassed by management and the union and then fired for organizing black workers, brought a gun to work and killed a foremen; then he went to the union hall and killed two union officials. Our Chicago group published a flyer calling for workers to rally to his defense. Not much came of it until... the League of Revolutionary Black Workers in Detroit reprinted our flyer in their paper. A Chrysler worker, James Johnson, responding to a history of unfair treatment including a suspension for refusing speedup, killed two foremen and a job setter, and was escorted from the plant saying "Long Live Ike Jernigan."

The League waged a mass campaign on Johnson's behalf, including rallies on the courthouse steps, while carrying out a legal defense based on a plea of temporary insanity. The high point of the trial came when the jury was led on a tour through Chrysler; it found for the defense, concluding that working at Chrysler was indeed enough to drive a person insane. (This was Detroit, and many people already knew that to be true.) Johnson was acquitted and sent to a mental hospital instead of to prison; as an added insult, Chrysler was ordered to pay him workmen's compensation. Such was the political power contained in the simple words, Recognize and Record.

The task of revolutionaries is not to organize the workers but to organize themselves – to discover those patterns of activity and forms of organization that have sprung up out of the struggle and that embody the new society, and to help them grow stronger, more confident, and more conscious of their direction. It is an essential contribution to the society of disciplined spontaneity, which for James was the definition of the new world.

The two works that follow illustrate James's worldview. *The Invading Socialist Society* was published in 1947 under the authorship of James, F. Forest (Raya Dunayevskaya) and Ria Stone (Grace Lee Boggs) as part of a discussion within the Trotskyist Fourth International. Inevitably it bears the marks of its birth, and some readers will be put off by the unfamiliar names and context. That would be unfortunate. As James wrote in his preface to the 1962 edition, "The reader can safely ignore or not bother himself about the details of these polemics, because *The Invading Socialist Society* is one of the key documents, in fact, in my opinion it is the fundamental document" of his political tendency. I shall not attempt to list its main points, but merely urge readers to note the astonishing degree to which it anticipated subsequent events, including the French General Strike of 1968 and the Polish Solidarity of 1980, which together marked the transcendence of the old vanguard party by the politicized nation, and the collapse of the Soviet Union and its satellites, and with it the collapse of the illusion that there ever existed more than one world system.

The second document, "Every Cook Can Govern," published in 1956 and written for a general audience, was equally prophetic. It is short enough, and rather than attempt to list its main points, I urge readers to read it bearing in mind the counterposing of representative and direct democracy that became so important to SNCC and other components of the New Left of the 1960s (best described in chapter 14 of *Ready for Revolution: The Life and Struggles of Stokely Carmichael* by Stokely Carmichael and Ekwueme Michael Thelwell).

Together, these two works represent the principal themes that run through James's life: implacable hostility toward all "condescending saviors" of the working class, and undying faith in the power of ordinary people to build a new world.

The Invading Socialist Society

C.L.R. James and Raya Dunayevskaya

1947

Preface to the 2nd Edition

C.L.R. JAMES

This pamphlet by the Johnson-Forest Tendency was published in 1947. The Johnson-Forest Tendency was a grouping in the Trotskyist movement which split off from the Socialist Workers Party in 1940 and went with what became the Workers Party. However, inside the Workers Party, the movement found it necessary to clarify its positions, not only against the empirical and eclectic jumps of Max Shachtman; we found it imperative to clarify our positions against those of Trotsky, positions which the Socialist Workers Party was repeating with ritual emphasis. It was in the course of doing this that in 1947 we published *The Invading Socialist Society*. But precisely our serious attitude to the fundamentals of Marxism led us to leave the happy-go-lucky improvisations of the Workers Party, and in 1948, to return to the Socialist Workers Party. This brief explanation will serve to place the document historically, and also to explain to the reader, the many polemical references to contemporary Marxist wraiths such as Shachtman, Muniz, and one who wrote under the now-forgotten name of Germain.

The reader can safely ignore or not bother himself about the details of these polemics, because *The Invading Socialist Society* is one of the key documents, in fact, in my opinion it is the fundamental document, of the Johnson-Forest Tendency, among the increasing number of its documents circulating under the heading of "Facing Reality."

Why do we consider this document so important for the comprehension of contemporary politics as to be worth reprinting? And so necessary for the understanding of the Marxist movement? The reason is as follows: it was in this document that for the first time we broke with the Trotskyist doctrine that the Stalinist parties were mere "tools of the Kremlin." As far as we know this was not only central to the Trotskyist doctrine but was universally held by the majority of Marxists and political analysts of the period.

The analysis of Stalinism and the Stalinist parties dominated Marxist thought of that period. What we said was that the Stalinist parties were not "tools of the Kremlin," but were an organic product of the mode of capitalism at this stage. Briefly to summarize the argument: the capitalistic monopolists could no longer control and direct capitalism and the working class. By this time, the Second International was utterly discredited and could no longer perform this function. The situation was ripe for the revolutionary party to lead the revolting workers. But this the Stalinist parties could not and would not do. By this time they had been innoculated with the doctrine that socialism consisted of the nationalization of private property. The idea that the emancipation of the proletariat would only be the work of the proletariat itself had been sternly repressed. Yet the bankruptcy of each national bourgeoisie was obvious. Each Stalinist party, therefore, aiming at power in its own country, supported the Moscow bureaucracy, waiting for the moment when the Red Army, militarily, and the nationalized economy, productively, would defeat the bourgeois state and open the way to Stalinist power.

That is the reason for the emphatic print in which we stated the political conclusions that we drew (page 112).

I. It is the task of the Fourth International to drive as clear a line between bourgeois nationalization and proletarian nationalization as the revolutionary Third International drove between bourgeois democracy and proletarian democracy.

II. The strategic orientation is the unification of proletarian struggle on an international scale as exemplified in the struggle for the Socialist United States of Europe.

The Johnson-Forest Tendency, becoming "Facing Reality," and finding the necessity of reprinting document after early document. reprints *The Invading Socialist Society* (a phrase we adopted from Engels) with particular awareness that for those who wish to understand the developments among the anti-Stalinist political Marxists, this is the place to begin.

It took us many years of hard work to arrive once more at the conclusion that:

> The mode of production of material life conditions the social, political and intellectual life process in general. It is not the consciousness of men that determines their being, but, on the contrary, their social being that determines their consciousness. (Preface to *The Critique of Political Economy* by Karl Marx.)

CHAPTER I

World War II and Social Revolution

One of Trotsky's last contributions to the Fourth International was a hypothetical prognosis of social development if the world revolution failed to come during or immediately after the war. Contrary to the belief of all the incurable Mensheviks and the panic stricken, this failure of the revolution was not, and could not have been conceived by Trotsky, of all people, metaphysically, as a point in time, one month, six months, two years. It was a dialectical forecast of a stage in the development of the international class struggle. If, in the crisis that Trotsky foresaw, the bourgeoisie could restore economic stability and its social domination over the proletariat, then he could not conceive another situation in which the proletariat could conquer.

In 1938 when Trotsky posed the question stated above, he drew the conclusion that, given the failure of the world revolution, the evolution of Russia might prove in retrospect to be the social basis for a new evaluation of the laws of scientific socialism. Russia remains, the world revolution has not conquered, and as a result in every section of the International, from the I.E.C. downwards the process of re-evaluation is taking place.

As far back as 1941 the W.P. Minority (Johnson-Forest), believing with Trotsky that under no circumstances could bourgeois relations of production save society from barbarism after the impending crisis, revised the official Russian position in the light of the present stage of development of capitalism, statification of production, and the consequent deepening of the mass revolutionary struggle. The W.P. Majority, (Shachtmanites), revised the whole Marxist-Leninist-Trotskyist strategy in the light of the Russian degeneration. The official Fourth International, under the blows of the "delayed" revolution, has continued to seek theoretical stability in the "progressive character" of the degenerated workers' state or to use its recurrent phrase "the dual character of the bureaucracy." Where the Kremlin and the Red Army advance, there the revolution has advanced. Where they retreat, there the revolution has retreated. Where Trotsky saw the nationalization of production as the last remaining conquest of proletarian power, the Fourth International today accepts nationalization of production as a stage in revolutionary development even if the revolution itself is brutally suppressed. Where Trotsky saw the Russian proletariat as dependent upon the impetus of the revolution from the proletariat outside, the I.E.C. sees as progressive the incorporation of millions from outside Russia into the totalitarian grip of the Russian bureaucracy.

A. TROTSKY 1940, GERMAIN 1947

The first thing to be done once and for all is to destroy Germain's illusion that he is interpreting Trotsky's positions of 1939. Trotsky in 1939 believed that the bureaucracy of the workers' state would give an "impulse" to revolutionary action among the oppressed masses in the areas it invaded in order to create a basis for itself. But this achieved, its Bonapartist tendencies would then assert themselves and crush the revolutionary masses. As he proved unmistakably, this is what happened in Poland and was posed in Finland in 1939.

Events at the end of the war took an entirely different course. The Russian Army did not call upon workers and peasants to revolt in order to create a basis for the bureaucracy. For country after country in Eastern Europe, Germain repeats with wearisome insistence: "The approach of the Red Army unloosed a revolutionary upheaval." Undoubtedly many workers and peasants in Eastern Europe believed that Stalin's army was revolutionary. But it was the break-down of bourgeois society which unloosed the revolutionary upheaval not only in Poland and Rumania, but in Italy, the Philippines and Paris. In reality, the agents of the bureaucracy carried on a systematic campaign against all the revolutionary elements in Poland before, during and after the uprising. The Russian army, the vanguard of the counter-revolution, in collaboration with British imperialism, took pains to have the Warsaw proletariat, the vanguard of the European revolution, destroyed by the Nazi army. Russia kept Marshal Paulus and the German Junkers in reserve against what it called "a repetition of 1918 in Germany." Ilya Ehrenberg, special propagandist for the European theatre, led the Stalinist pack in an unprecedented international vilification of the German people, which reached its height in the declaration that if the German workers made a revolution and **approached the Red Army as brothers**, they would be shot down like dogs.

Despite this, the Russian Army found revolutionary formations in existence, Soviets, factory committees, and militias. There was no bourgeoisie and industry was in the hands of the workers. The Russian Army arrested, deported or murdered the revolutionary elements. It destroyed step by step the traditional Polish workers' parties and created new ones in its own image. It restored remnants of the Polish bourgeoisie to positions of power and created what Germain admits is a bourgeois state. Germain admits that the Russian Army sanctioned nationalization because where it entered, a virtual nationalization had already taken place. Then he coolly informs us, "The activity of the Stalinist bureaucracy inevitably exhibits a double character: on the one hand it has facilitated [facilitated, if you please] in however limited a measure, nationalization, agrarian reform, the establishment of factory committees, etc.," on the other hand it established the police regime. Then he dares us to deny "the dual character of bureaucratic intervention." (*Fourth International*, Feb. 1947.)

Whoever wishes to advance this infatuated inversion of great historical events may do so but he will do so on his own authority and under his own name. He will not in our movement get away with this as "Trotsky's position."

We have declared and will declare again our opposition to Trotsky's policy of 1940. But before attacking a policy, it is necessary to understand it. It is even more necessary to do so when defending it. In 1940 Trotsky argued:

1) that the defeat of Russia could mean the dismemberment of the U.S.S.R., and give imperialism a further long lease of life;

2) that only the defeat of the bureaucracy by the revolution would preserve state property in the U.S.S.R.;

3) that the Stalinist parties abroad would desert the Kremlin regime and capitulate to their own bourgeoisies.

Which of these judgments does Germain still defend? He does not even face them.

1) He and his school are probably the only persons in the world who believe that the imperialism of today, shattered beyond repair, can have a long lease on life by the dismemberment of Russia. This indeed is faith in capitalism.

2) Further, if we understand the 1939 Trotsky at all, if we watch the iron laws of economic development today and observe the barbarism that is eating away at bourgeois society, the patching up of the universal ruin of another war could not reverse but would accelerate the movement to the nationalization not only of national but continental economies. But Germain continues to agitate himself about the prospects of capitalist restoration after a new war by millionaire collective-farmers.

3) Finally, it is clear to all (again except Germain) that the Stalinist parties are tied to the Kremlin by roots far deeper than Trotsky believed. They did not join their national bourgeoisie during the war. They did not collapse and abdicate to the Fourth International the leadership of millions. We thus have today in fact a more complicated relation of fundamental forces and perspectives than those on which Trotsky based his positions.

To these fundamental problems Germain has his answer ready: "planned economy" and the "dual character of the bureaucracy." There is not a trace, not one drop of Marxism, of the dialectical method, in this.

Socialism in a Single Country is Dead

What is so terrible is that fundamental concepts are being changed, altered, transformed, shifted around, without the theoreticians ever stopping to think of what they are doing. If is proceeding, for the most part, unconsciously and empirically.

It is still our common belief that we subscribe to the Leninist analysis of imperialism, as the struggle of conflicting imperialisms for the re-division of the world. It is obvious that the I.K.D. and Shachtman do not believe this. For them there is only one significant imperialist state in the Leninist sense of the word. That is American imperialism. (It is ridiculous to consider Britain as a serious competitor with the United States.) They call Russia "bureaucratic imperialism" whatever that may mean, but this has no scientific relation to American imperialism, i.e., a relation within the capital–labor antagonism in the context of the world market.

But Germain also has completely reorganized in his own mind the foundation of our period. **For him also the world market is similarly destroyed**. For him also there is only one imperialist state. Wall Street is engaged in a struggle not with another imperialism but with a degenerated workers' state that can be transitional to socialism. Thus the one world trust aims at dominating the rest of the world. There is no imperialist rivalry between American imperialism and the U.S.S.R. There is the capitalist enemy and its projected victim.

Thus both Germain and Shachtman destroy all our conceptions of the laws of the world market and the domination of the capital–labor relation by these laws. It is not only possible but perfectly legitimate to take these tremendous theoretical steps. But it is absolutely intolerable that such tremendous theoretical re-evaluations should take place without their being clearly stated and the conclusions drawn.

It is when the normal trade connections of the world-market are destroyed that the law of value imposes itself with unrestrained ferocity. Russia must fight for world domination or perish. It is subjected to all the laws of the world-market. Socialism in a single country is dead even for Stalin. All theories built on this are also dead.

The bourgeoisie sees Stalinist Russia, nationalized property, as "attacking the capitalist world." Germain sees nationalized property as "defending" itself. Thereby Germain is unable to reaffirm what the bourgeoisie seeks to destroy – the revolutionary unity of the world proletariat, the only solution to the contemporary barbarism.

The greatest enemy of the United States is not Stalinist Russia (this is a purely bourgeois conception). Its greatest enemy is at home, the American proletariat in alliance with the world revolution. But in the new necessity for world rule, equally, the greatest enemy of Russian domination is not American imperialism but the Russian proletariat. As in the moment of victory it collaborated with Hitler to destroy the revolutionary proletariat of Warsaw, so Stalinism will and must collaborate with American imperialism for the maintenance of the condition of their joint existence – the suppression of the world proletarian revolution. It was possible (possible, if wrong) at one time to speculate about the revolutionary aspect of the bureaucracy, its preservation of a planned economy to save Russia from dismemberment and ruin and the consequent strengthening of imperialism. Those days are over. Today the task is to save the proletariat from a power which contends with by no means inferior forces for world mastery.

This is not a question of Germany or defense of Russia. Germain, viewing all historical development through the eyes of the theory of the degenerated workers' state, is eating away at the theoretical foundations of our movement, i.e., the revolutionary mobilization of the proletariat as the sole solution to all the problems of the contemporary barbarism. We join Germain in holding off Shachtman and the other guerrillas in order to face him with the origins and consequences of his utterly false political position.

Lenin and Socialism

The struggle for socialism is the struggle for proletarian democracy. Proletarian democracy is not the crown of socialism. It is its basis. Proletarian democracy is not the result of socialism. Socialism is the result of proletarian democracy. To the degree that the proletarian mobilizes itself and the great masses of the people, the socialist revolution is advanced. The proletariat mobilizes itself as a self-acting force through its own committees, unions, parties and other organizations. This is not the "Russian question." It is Marxism. Lenin based everything, yes, Comrade Germain, everything on this.

> The civil war against the bourgeoisie is a war which is **democratically** organized and waged by the poor masses

> against the propertied minority. The civil war is also a war, and consequently must inevitably put 'force' in the place of right. But force ... cannot be realized without a democratic organization of the army and the '**rear.**' The civil war first of all and at once expropriates banks, factories, railways, large agricultural estates, etc. But it is precisely **for this very purpose** of expropriation that it is imperative to introduce the election by the people of all the officials and the army officers; to accomplish a **complete fusion** of the army, which wages war against the bourgeoisie, with the masses of the population; to introduce complete democracy in the matter of the control of food supplies, of production and distribution, etc. ... But this aim can be attained **neither** from a purely military **nor** economic **nor** political standpoint without a simultaneous introduction and propagation of democracy among our troops and at our rear – an introduction and propagation which will develop in the course of that war. We tell the masses now . ... 'You must lead and you will lead a really democratic war against the bourgeoisie and for the purpose of actually carrying out democracy and socialism'. (*Bolsheviks and the World War*, pp. 227–228.)

The same principle applies to the self-determination of nations.

> Without actually organizing the relations between the nations on a democratic basis – and hence without granting freedom of secession – there can be no civil war of the workers and the toiling masses of all nations against the bourgeoisie. (*Ibid.*, p. 228.)

We shall pursue Germain remorselessly until he faces this issue and answers.

The Commune, the first decisively proletarian revolution, nationalized nothing. For Marx, "The great social measure of the Commune was its own working existence," its democratic mobilization of the masses of the people. In the 1917 revolution, the socialist revolution, we have precisely the same theory and therefore the same practice. In 1917 Lenin attacked mercilessly not merely nationalization but confiscation. "The vital thing will be not so much confiscation of capitalist property as the establishment of universal, all-embracing workers' control over the capitalists and their possible supporters." And then, Comrade Germain, note this: "Confiscation alone will lead us nowhere..." Lenin left no room for ambiguity on this question. He declared that the Bolsheviks never used the term "workers' control" except in association with the dictatorship of the proletariat, "always putting it after the latter (by which) we thereby make plain what state we have in mind."

State control – that was "a bourgeois-reformist phrase, in essence a purely Cadet formula..." The Junker-capitalist state in Germany during war time was exercising complete class control over the economy and it meant "military penal labor" for the workers. For Marx and Lenin, the regime transitional to socialism was the dictatorship of the proletariat, the power of the working class, not the regime of nationalized property. For Lenin "the fundamental idea which runs like a red thread through all of Marx's works" is that "the democratic republic is the nearest approach to the dictatorship to the proletariat." The democratic republic with its opportunity for mass mobilizations, not bourgeois nationalization of property. This explains Lenin's merciless enmity to the bourgeois regulation of economic life as a whole "according to a certain general plan." In fact, the leaders of the October Revolution specifically excluded confiscation of property from their immediate program. They were concerned with something else – the democratic, i.e., self-mobilization of the masses.

For Lenin the solution to the **economic** ills of ruined Russia was **not** nationalization of property but the release of the energies of the people. This was and is so profoundly revolutionary so opposed to **bourgeois** conceptions that even today, the words stare us in the face and we cannot understand them.

> In our opinion, in order to mitigate the untold burdens and miseries of the war, in order to heal the terrible wounds inflicted on the people by the war, revolutionary democracy is necessary, revolutionary measures are needed, of the kind described in the example of the allocation of dwellings in the interests of the poor. We must proceed in exactly the same way, in both town and country, with regard to foodstuffs, clothes, boots, and so forth, and in the country with regard to the land, etc. For the administration of the state in this spirit we can immediately set up a state apparatus of about ten million, if not twenty million people – an apparatus

> unknown to any capitalist country. We alone can create such an apparatus, for we are assured of the complete and devoted sympathy of the vast majority of the population. This apparatus we alone can create, because we have class conscious workers, disciplined by a long capitalist 'apprenticeship' (not for naught did we serve apprenticeship to capitalism), workers who are capable of forming a workers' militia and of gradually enlarging it (beginning to enlarge it immediately) into a people's militia. The class conscious workers must lead, but they can draw into the work of administration the real masses of the toiling oppressed. (*Selected Works*, Vol. VI, p. 274.)

Confiscation Will Solve Nothing

Is Germain prepared to subscribe to this program or not? Is he prepared to tell the French workers today that mere nationalization or even confiscation will solve nothing? He cannot do it because his Russian position stands over him like a janissary with sword drawn.

For Lenin administration of the state by the proletariat was the same as administration of the economy. Without a break the passage passes on to the solution of economic problems.

> The most important thing is to inspire the oppressed and the toilers with confidence in their own strength, to show them in practice that they can and must themselves undertake **a correct**, strictly orderly and organized distribution of bread, food, milk, clothing, dwellings, and so forth, **in the interests of the poor**. Without this, Russia **cannot** be saved from collapse and ruin; whereas an honest, courageous and universal move to hand over the administration to the proletarians and semi-proletarians will arouse such unprecedented revolutionary enthusiasm among the masses, will so multiply the forces of the people in combating their miseries, that much that seemed impossible to our old, narrow, bureaucratic forces will become practicable for the forces of the millions and millions of the masses when they **begin to work for themselves**, and not under the whip, for the capitalist, the master, the official.

The most important thing is to tell the workers what is to be done and that only they can do it. You can see the same in every line of these pamphlets.

> Only then shall we be able to see what untapped forces of resistance to capitalism are latent in the people; only then will what Engels calls 'latent socialism' be made apparent; only then shall we find that for every ten thousand open or concealed enemies of the power of the working class, who manifest themselves either by action or by passive resistance, a million new fighters will arise, who until then had been politically dormant, languishing in poverty and despair, having lost faith in themselves as human beings, in their right to live, in the possibility that they too might be served by the whole force of the modern centralized state and that their detachments of proletarian militia might be fully trusted and called upon to take part in the immediate, direct, day-to-day work of administration of the state. (*Selected Works*, Vol. VI, p. 287.)

As concrete, revolutionary policy for the masses to act upon, Lenin, with his incomparable concreteness, was placing before them nothing more than the theoretical conclusions of Marx, that the solution to the problems of capital accumulation was the human solution.

> It becomes a question of life and death for society to adapt the mode of production to the normal functioning of this law. Modern industry, indeed, compels society, under penalty of death, to replace the detail-worker of today, crippled by life-long repetition of one and the same trivial operation, and thus reduced to a mere fragment of a man, by the fully-developed individual fit for a variety of labors, ready to face any change of production, and to whom the different social functions he performs are but so many modes of giving free scope to his own natural and acquired powers. (*Capital*, Vol. 1, p. 534.)

The whole debate about nationalization should be mercilessly swept aside with the brutality with which Lenin swept it aside.[1] Today, in 1947, it is no more than a means, and, with bourgeois and Stalinists, a deliberate means of blinding the masses to the need for their own self-mobilization. And Lenin was Lenin and Trotskyism was Bolshevism precisely because it was the ruthless enemy of all that impeded this self-mobilization.

1 Later we shall take up the question of the actual use of the slogan in 1947.

Today we are far, far beyond the stage for which Lenin was writing. The crisis, as Trotsky foresaw it, and as we can see it today, demands that the International speak to the masses in a manner infinitely surpassing in boldness and range the Lenin of 1917–1918. Where is it? Look at the press of the International. In words and resolutions it attacks the opportunists (and feebly enough); concretely, it cannot demonstrate its difference. Far better if it were, in every country, to do nothing more for three months than reprint week after week the *State and Revolution, The Threatening Catastrophe, Will the Bolsheviks Retain State-Power?, The Immediate Tasks of the Soviet Government,* Trotsky's *Transitional Program* and above all the discussions that preceded it. The masses would learn more than we have taught them for the past year and we would also. And yet today even these are inadequate.

Under our eyes, the masses, the fountain of all Marxist theory, are creating the basis of the Fourth International. But to see this, Germain will have to tear himself from his mesmerized contemplation of degeneration in Russia and grapple with the regeneration of the proletariat, with the stages of development of our movement and its present situation, shaped not by Russian degeneration but by world capitalism.

B. THE HISTORICAL ROLE OF THE FOURTH INTERNATIONAL

In 1942 the reactionary laws of the American bourgeoisie made it necessary for Trotskyist tendencies in the United States to disaffiliate organizationally from the Fourth International. That, however, cannot prevent our subscription to political ideas and an interest in their expression in organizations and tendencies. It is in this sense that we write here of the Fourth International.

Germain, secure, in his exposition of "Trotsky's positions," has no need to show in precise terms what organic changes, if any, have taken place in world imperialism since Trotsky wrote in 1940. Exactly similar is his method with the laws of political development. The Fourth International was small in 1939. It is still small in 1947. The masses are more (or less) revolutionary as the case may be, etc. We must redouble our energies, etc., etc. But how exactly does the Fourth International in 1947 differ from the Fourth International in 1939? What new conception can it have of itself and its tasks in the light of the developments between 1940 and 1947? Germain does not even ask himself these questions.

In the Manifesto of the Communist International, 1919, Trotsky states:

> If the First International presaged the future course of development and indicated its paths; if the Second International gathered and organized millions of workers; then the Third International is the International of open mass action, the International of revolutionary realization, the International of the deed.

We have to examine this concentrated generalization, see what it means, place each International in relation to its period and arrive at what the Fourth International means today. That is the historic continuity of our movement, not the "dual character of the bureaucracy."

The First International was founded in an epoch in which small bourgeois production predominated. Marx, basing himself upon the most advanced stage and tendencies of the capital–labor relation of those days, fought for the revolutionary mobilization of the proletariat on the basis of unifying its economic and political struggles. He had to struggle against conspiratorial Blanquists and Anarchists for the systematic politicalization of the everyday proletarian struggle.

The Second International was founded on the realization in life of the theoretical perspectives for which Marx fought in the first International. The development of capitalism itself had solidified, unified and differentiated the proletariat from the rest of the nation, and clarified its role. Its clearly marked place in the social structure of advancing capitalism dictated the strategy of the Second International, the mobilization of the proletariat for revolutionary action. But the development of imperialism with its super-profits created the political democracy and social legislation which dissolved the unified social action of the proletariat into an amorphous mass of electors drowned in the petty-bourgeois swamp.

The dialectical development is now manifested with extraordinary clarity. If the *revolutionary perspectives* of the First International were the *concrete* foundation of the Second, the revolutionary perspectives of the Second International became in time the concrete foundations of the Third. The Third International was founded on the actual revolutionary upheaval of the masses, the October Revolution, mass general strikes, Soviets, and armed demonstrations on a European scale. Capitalism had produced these just as it produced the foundations at each stage of the previous labor organization. And at each successive stage the degeneration of the proletarian party not only imitates capitalism but must take on **to a greater degree** the contradictions which are rending capitalism.

Beginning with 1933, Fascism, the bureaucratic control by the state of all aspects of life, becomes the political method of the bourgeoisie. Government even in democratic countries maintains only the form of legislative procedure and becomes in reality government by executive decree. The labor movement everywhere and the Third International above all complete a strictly parallel degeneration.

As in previous stages, with the degeneration of the labor movement, society itself culminates in social catastrophe, the series of defeated revolutions which preceded World War II, the war itself, and the insoluble crisis of the present. But here, the logical development of the International becomes of fundamental importance for us to understand our own present and our own future. The theoretical perspectives of the Third International, expressed most concretely by Lenin for Russia in the articles quoted, will logically become the concrete actual foundation of the Fourth.

In 1864, the revolution aimed at achieving social emancipation in the future. Today, revolution must begin with social emancipation. No conceivable force exists in the world to begin the regeneration of society except the emancipated proletariat. The Fourth International must tell the workers that only the free scope of their "own natural and acquired powers" and the "latent socialism" of their class can satisfy their most elementary needs. This is the theoretical basis of the revolutionary international of 1947. Where Marx fought to unify political and economic struggles, today, long past that stage, the Fourth International has to aim at the unification in the struggle of the national units of the proletariat, for the **international reconstruction of economic life**.

The emancipation must be social.

Only the complete social transformation of man as a productive force can begin to cope with the ruin, economic, political and moral, to which bourgeois society has reduced and is still further reducing the world.

The emancipation must be international.

1939–1947, and particularly 1945–1947, have demonstrated to the whole world, and particularly to the European proletariat, that the old national economies are shattered beyond repair. This was not so in 1940. The United States, the U.S.S.R. and the colonial countries are knit into an almost inextricable fabric with Europe. The world moves as a unit.

The tasks of the Fourth International have therefore undergone a qualitative change. Its most remote theories of 1940 have become in 1947 practical necessities for millions. Neither in theory nor in practice does Germain show any grasp of this. He is too tied up in "property" and "nationalization" to perform the first task of today. It is to examine and establish to what degree the objective movement and subjective expression of the proletariat correspond to the objective needs of society and the subjective claims of his organization. Germain's treatment of this, where it exists, is superficial and impressionistic. For the Johnson-Forest tendency the correspondence is established and is the greatest political factor of our time. With the world socialist revolution the history of humanity will begin. And that is precisely what is already shaking the world. Vast millions of men are not thinking or acting as in the old days. They are flexing themselves for a leap that has become imperative for them – the leap from the realm of capitalist necessity into the realm of social freedom. This today is revolutionary politics. The revolutionary writer who does not know this, scratches only on the surface – and then begins to slip backward.

C. THE MASS MOVEMENT TODAY

The mass movement today is not essentially the product of the war. Its first appearance is in France in 1934, after one year's experience by Europe of the barbarism and degradation of Fascism.

In the space of three or four months after the June 1936 strikes in France *four million workers* join the French trade union movement "lining up for the class struggle." In Spain the workers revolted with a violence and decisiveness never seen in any previous revolution. But it is in the U.S.A. that the phenomenon can be most instructively observed. Within two years the American proletariat creates the C.I.O., which in ten years becomes the most powerful social force in the nation, an achievement rarely exceeded in the history of the proletariat.

The victories of Hitler seemed to hurl back this world-wide mobilization of the proletariat. At the first check he received in 1941, the proletariat began the struggle on a higher plane. The resistance movements were nothing less than a higher stage of the self-mobilization of the proletariat as leader of the nation now deserted by the bourgeoisie.

Today this mass movement continues in the rush to join the Communist Parties. Nowhere in the writings of Germain and his co-thinkers is it possible to find a single paragraph which recognizes that this is the greatest social phenomenon of the age, the proletarian mobilization corresponding to the degeneration of bourgeois society.

Tomorrow if the Communist Parties in Western Europe should seriously undertake a series of decisive actions with the conquest of power as the open aim, the millions would pour into it as they poured into the unions in 1936. This is in no sense a national or Western European phenomenon. In Japan, in Indonesia, in Shanghai, and in West Africa, there is the same type of self-mobilization. It has been growing with advances and retreats for thirteen years.

The French and Italian workers of today are not the Russian workers of 1917 seizing factories chaotically and trying to run them individually. They have been trained and disciplined in a more advanced school of capitalism, in a more complex world, in a society where social collapse and barbarism are very close. In the tightly-knit network of Western Europe they are profoundly aware of the interdependence of the economy, of the diminishing opposition between national and international economy, between national and international politics, between peace and war, and the need for centralized organization.

In the Resolution on the role of the Communist Party at the Second Congress of the Communist International, Zinoviev stated that the former subdivisions of the workers' movement into the three forms, party, union, and co-operative, had exhausted itself. The new forms of the dictatorship of the proletariat were party, soviet and industrial unions. The whole resolution is built around the idea that even "on the day of the conquest of power the Communist Party constitutes only a fraction of the working class." This was the axis on which Lenin worked for Russia and for the whole of Western Europe. What we are seeing in France and Italy shows how far beyond 1919 we are.

Any revolutionary party today which initiated actions for the conquest of power would rally such a membership as would reduce to the vanishing point the organizational difference between vanguard and masses, party, Soviet and union. The revolutionary party will not be only a "fraction" of the working-class. In a country like France at the moment of the conquest of power, we can well see practically every member of the organized labor movement and millions of the petty-bourgeoisie as members of the revolutionary party.[2] For Shachtman and such, all this is stratospheric "theory." Yet it is only with this in mind (and not revolutionary waves which were unloosed by the Red Army) that we shall begin to see the catastrophic role played by the Red Army in Eastern Europe and the lessons for today.

In 1917 the February and October Revolutions gave the impetus to the European revolution precisely because of the backwardness of Russia. In 1944 the revolutionary mobilization of the masses in the Eastern European countries under the impending defeat of Germany was historically due to be the signal and example for such a mobilization in Western Europe as would have put the 1917–1923 revolutions in the shade. It is this the Kremlin, deliberately and farsightedly counter-revolutionary, destroyed. Could Anglo-American imperialism have held the populations of those countries down? Look at the rest of the world and judge. We would have had a repetition of Greece (Greece which Germain so grievously misunderstands) in every country in Eastern Europe; the Middle East aflame and a movement in Western Europe to which even the present unprecedented self-mobilization of the masses would have been merely a prelude.

Where the Red Army Has Not Passed

The analysis must be taken to its conclusion, as our teachers taught

2 How ridiculous all the disputes about the dictatorship of the party over the masses already begin to appear!

us to do and because today historical development takes all processes to their logical conclusion. Already in the Spanish Civil War in 1936 the French proletariat was seething with the consciousness that it was necessary to go to the aid of the Spanish proletariat. All through the war the elements of international action particularly in North Italy and the Balkans, existed. Stalinism corrupted and destroyed it when it destroyed the revolution. Yet today the self-mobilization of the masses in Italy and France on a national scale has reached such a stage that given serious action of any kind, always decisive for proletarian consciousness, it is bound to overflow the national boundaries.

In the *Critique of the Gotha Program* (1875) Marx drew attention to the fact that thirty years before in the Communist Manifesto, he had warned that the class struggle is national "in form" only but not in content. In 1873 he had taken it further. Referring to the death of the First International he had declared that "The international activity of the working class does not by any means depend on the existence of the International Workingmen's Association." Had Churchill's plan for the Anglo-American invasion of Eastern Europe been successful, the revolutionary masses of Europe, despite internal divisions, would have faced on an international scale one enemy, Anglo-American imperialism. That initial impulse has been beheaded, and corrupted by the Kremlin bureaucracy and its army.

Included in this terrible set-back for the revolution is Germany, Eastern and Western. In Belgrade, Sofia, and above all, in Warsaw, the German proletarian revolution was undermined. Those bourgeois commentators who declare that but for the Red Army, all Europe would have been communist today, not only speak far more wisely than they know but have infinitely more grasp of the truth than all the "Marxism" of Germain's theses. And as recompense for all this we have the barely concealed defeatism by Germain in the oft-reiterated prospect of "structural assimilation to the U.S.S.R.," including Eastern Germany. And to conclude, he gives us the truly preposterous piece of capitalism in a single country – "the growth of the productive forces" in those ruined, plundered, tortured, starving countries of Eastern Europe, the most stricken areas of a stricken and collapsing continent, which in another page Germain will assure us must achieve the Socialist United States of Europe or perish.

All the lamentations over the fate of the German proletariat and the need for economic recovery before it can once more take its place in the revolutionary struggle are the most pitiful capitulation to bourgeois ideology and the direct result of a false method of analysis. But for its ghastly experience with the Red Army, Germany today might have only one party, a revolutionary party of millions. But even given the present state of Germany, the revolutionary proletariat of France and Italy, dragging with them the Ruhr workers, can at one stroke lift the German people to their feet again.

Entangled in the meshes of his concepts of bureaucracy, Germain has cut himself off from understanding the dynamics of the mass movement today. It will have periods of lull, retreat and even defeat. But its main outlines and the course of development are already clear. It is a world-wide phenomenon. The unprecedented movement of the Japanese proletariat is only superficially different in kind. There is being prepared in the United States (and the bourgeoisie is frantic in fear of it) a self-mobilization of the great mass of the nation which will assume a national and international scope that will shake the globe. Wherever the Red Army has *not* passed, there this movement exists.

We are not formalists. The logical deduction is for us only the guide to proof by practice – in this case empirical examination. Germain may say that more or less he agrees. But if he does, that would only be another example of the dilemma in which he finds himself, between his revolutionary strivings and the theoretical stranglehold of the "dual character of the bureaucracy." For if he saw the mass movement of the proletariat as he ought to see it, he would recognize and declare and build policy on the fact that the extension of the power of the Kremlin constitutes the growth of the most determined, the most skillful, the most experienced, the most conscious enemy of precisely this self-mobilization of the masses.

D. THE COMMUNIST PARTIES IN WESTERN EUROPE

1. The Proletarian and Revolutionary Character of the Stalinist Parties

When the masses in one country move, the world theory of Bolshevism leaps forward. Now today we have two and a half million in one Italian Communist Party, before the seizure of power. Europe has seen nothing like this since the Crusades. It is here that are concentrated all the problems of our age.[3]

Germain does not see here a new stage of the mass movement, and therefore the new stage of theoretical advance. He is busy instead – defeating Shachtman.

The relation with World War I will show the new stage. After World War I there was a tremendous movement of the masses into the Trade Union movement. Said Trotsky in 1919:

> The workers join the trade unions solely for the sake of immediate gains' reply the conciliators. This theory is false from beginning to end. The great influx of workers into the trade unions is elicited not by petty, day-to-day questions, but by the colossal fact of the World War. The working masses, not only the top layers but the lowest depths as well, are roused and alarmed by the greatest historical upheaval. Each individual proletarian has sensed to a never equaled degree his helplessness in the face of the mighty imperialist machine. The urge to establish ties, the urge to unification and consolidation of forces has manifested itself with unprecedented power. Hence flows the surge of millions of workers into the trade unions or into the Soviets of Deputies, i.e., into such organizations as do not demand political preparation but represent the most general and most direct expression of the proletarian class struggle. [*The First Five Years of the Communist International*, p. 73]

The workers today are aware of the tremendous problems involved in the overthrow of bourgeois society. They seek a philosophy of life, a place, an organization, a social force which will not only be "the direct expression of the proletarian class struggle" but the direct force with which to rebuild society. In Indonesia and Indo-China, slight as is the proletarian base, we see the same total mobilization. It is only the occupation forces in Japan that impede a similar manifestation. The

3 The membership of the Italian Communist Party is said to be a "book" membership. The observation is without sense. For the Italian workers the party was a legend, the party of Lenin and Trotsky. They joined it for action. Without action they fall away. Trotsky's remarks on the unions in 1919 are sufficient to expose any superficial analysis of the Italian people and the Communist Party in Italy.

genuine mass organization of the American proletariat, the socially most advanced social entity the world has ever seen, will show that the Stalinism of the Stalinist parties is merely a subjective expression of the world proletariat, instinctively unifying and consolidating social forces in the face of dangers and tasks. This is the invading socialist society of our day.

The Proletariat Then and Now

As late as 1864 Marx's concrete economic program showed how closely he differentiated between the boldness of his theoretical conclusions and the concrete stage of economic development and its reflection in the revolutionary proletariat. Even this seemed to be mere Utopianism when the Commune erupted like a volcano and projected the proletariat itself far beyond his theories. Yet its strictly economic program is today ridiculous – one of the things which Marx details with great pride is the abolition of night-work for journeymen bakers.

The degeneration of the Second International consisted precisely in the fact that it separated what the Commune at a high moment had joined together, moderate economic content but a new political organization of the masses. The Second International placed militant trade unionism on one side and social legislation on the other. But in 1905 the Russian proletariat linked the two together in the Soviet which, became the pattern for revolutionary action from 1917 onwards. Yet in the consciousness of the workers, the Soviet still remained a form of political activity, proletarian politics, but essentially revolutionary activity against the bourgeoisie. Between 1923 and 1929 the failure of the world revolution and the stabilizing influence of American capital in Western Europe made it impossible for the backward Russian proletariat to give the Soviets that content (administration of the state and workers' control of production) which Lenin strove to instill into the Soviet form.

The failure of the world revolution reintroduced the old separation between economics and politics. The unions and the parties divided the economic and political struggle over the production and distribution of the surplus-value. With the increasing fall in the rate of profit and the increasing socialization of labor, and the disciplining, training and social education of the proletariat, this separation between economics and politics could not be long maintained. The proletariat received from Fascism a merciless subjective education in the integration of economics and politics which was not lost upon it.

Now, today, the proletariat, on a higher plane, has drawn the ultimate conclusion. Its revolt is not against politics and the distribution of the surplus-value. **The revolt is against value production itself**. It has made its own comprehension of the pivot on which the comprehension of political economy turns.

Be His Payment High or Low

From end to end of the world, the miners in Germany, in Britain, in the United States, in Russia do not seek merely higher pay ("be his payment high or low") or better working conditions. In peace or war, in summer or blizzards, they do not want to work in the mines at all. Every word from Japan shows that the Japanese workers aim at nothing less than the complete reorganization of society. The proletariat is not seeking as in the Commune a mere political form in which to work out the emancipation of labor, nor is it seeking as in the 1917–1923 Soviets a means for revolutionary politics, to overthrow private property. Its aims are greater. It seeks a complete transformation of the productive system.

The pivot of the whole science of political economy as Marx conceived it, his own special discovery, as he tells us in the first pages of *Capital*, was found in the dual character not of finished commodities on the market (Ricardo could get no further) but in the dual character of the labor that created them. Labor's fundamental, its eternally necessary function in all societies, past, present and future, was to create use-values. Into this organic function of all labor, capitalist production imposed the contradiction of producing value, and more particularly surplus-value. Within this contradiction is contained the necessity for the division of society into direct producers (workers) and rulers of society, into manual and intellectual laborers. On this class distinction rests the bourgeois distinction between economics and politics.

The proletariat in the advanced countries has now given notice that it is ready to solve these contradictions and abolish labor as "labor," as Marx used the term before 1848. It seeks to substitute instead a meaningful creative activity with a social aim as the end and the exercise of its natural and acquired faculties as the means.

Nations like the United States, Britain, France, and Germany could withdraw millions of men from production, feed them, clothe them, educate them, supply them with the weapons of destruction, transport them to the ends of the earth and maintain them for years. Today it is perfectly possible for the advanced nations by a self-mobilization of the population and modern methods of education to train and educate, technically and socially, all its able-bodied population between 16 and 35 without drawing them from labor for more than half the normal capitalist working day of 8 hours. Thus while within a decade civilization can be turned into a barbarous shambles, within a decade also there can be created such a social force for production and the democratic administration of things as Marx and Engels and even Lenin thought would come only in the second generation of socialism. The needs of the proletariat today are thus a direct response to the stage of development of capitalism itself.

The social and political education of the proletariat is on a corresponding scale. The world now moves from day to day by a series of gigantic convulsions. Men have to think in terms of global solutions. It is precisely the character of our age and the maturity of humanity that obliterates the opposition between theory and practice, between the intellectual preoccupations of the "educated" and of the masses. All the great philosophical concepts, from the nature of the physical universe (atomic energy) through the structure and function of productive systems (free enterprise, "socialism," or "communism"), the nature of government (the state versus the individual) to the destiny of man (can mankind survive?) these are no longer "theory," but are in the market-place, tied together so that they cannot be separated. matters on which the daily lives of millions upon millions depend.

The unending murders, the destruction of peoples, the bestial passions, the sadism, the cruelties and the lusts, all the manifestations of barbarism, of the last thirty years are unparalleled in history. But this barbarism exists only because nothing else can suppress the readiness for sacrifice, the democratic instincts and creative power of the great masses of the people.

The world revolution manifests itself not in the Red Army but in Palestine. The violence in Palestine is only secondarily Jewish. It is an indication of the stage of development of class antagonisms on a world scale and of the social temper of the working masses everywhere. The same holds true of the events in Indonesia, Indo-China. India, China, and Burma. These tell us what is the revolutionary potentiality of the proletariat in Britain, France, the United States and Holland.

The Surface of the Iceberg

Experience in the factories has shown that it is precisely fundamental solutions that workers are ready to listen to because fundamental questions are posed all around them both objectively and subjectively. The subjective factor, man as man and not as the slave of capital is now emerging as the decisive force in history and is organizing itself to correspond. The bourgeoisie in every country, but particularly in the United States has seen into this as far as it is possible for an alien class to see. Not only in highly organized investigations and reports, but, in journals costing nickels and dimes and sold to the proletariat in millions, the American bourgeoisie is shocked beyond measure at the incredible and apparently senseless behavior of the American proletariat. It confesses its fear that the proletariat will never again slave at the assembly line in the old way, and that it is social frustration, the cramping – of personality, of its "natural and acquired powers," the need for universality (not wages and higher standard of living) which are ruining the productivity of labor and driving the proletariat to repeated manifestations of hostility to the society. The condition is permanent. It is not French, it is not Italian, it is not Japanese, it is not Stalinist. It is proletarian and socialist, it has been developing since 1934, it is crushed to the ground only to leap forward again, broader and deeper, while the traditional organizations scurry in terror before it. Tomorrow it will be the United States, where the same type of mass mobilization, heaving out from the very depths of society will take place.

What the proletariat has shown so far is only the surface of the iceberg. Just as the Commune leapt above the level of European society, and the Soviets in 1905 created a political form undreamt of even by Lenin – so today the proletariat has not yet entered into its new creative period of political-economic organization. The production relations and the social and political problems of 1947 have created a need for solutions far beyond the modest beginning of Marx's day.

This is the social basis of the growth of the Stalinist parties. The Stalinist parties where this movement has taken concrete form are not political organizations in the old sense of the term. Behind the smoke-screen of democratic parliamentarism in France and Italy, they are social organizations. They symbolize the most profound mass revolt against capital that we have yet seen. They exercise a varying but substantial control in their own way over whole sections of the army, police, banks, production and distribution. They constitute a form of state power within the national state, dominating the private lives of citizens and the intellectual life of the country in all spheres. It appears as Stalinism in France and Italy. It may appear as an organization of the C.I.O. bureaucracy in the United States tomorrow. It calls itself Social-Democratic in Japan. But until the Fourth International recognizes these formations for what they are, and draws from them the full conclusions, draws the arrow to the head as Marx drew it before 1848, in 1864 and afterwards in 1871, as Lenin drew it in 1905 and again in 1917, and as Trotsky drew it in 1938, then just so long will the Fourth International remain unable to understand the modern proletariat and its own historical role.

2. The Bourgeois and Counter-Revolutionary Character of the Stalinist Parties

Shachtman attacks Trotsky's analysis of the Stalinist parties. He discovers that they are totalitarian parties. This theory is the most foolish of all Shachtman's theories. But the more Germain writes in "defense" of Trotsky's ideas the clearer if becomes that Germain does not even know what he is "defending."

Trotsky had a world conception. He never operated from the basis of Stalinism. When he said that the Fourth International would be leading millions at the end of the war or during the post-war, he was not "predicting," nor was he being "optimistic." Trotsky, strictly scientific, based his analysis on the bourgeois crisis driving the Stalinist parties to their national bourgeoisies. **He saw a repetition on a higher scale of 1914.**

It was the most serious of all his errors.[4] This is why he foresaw at a certain stage the political isolation of Stalinist Russia, and the emergence of the revolutionary masses under the banner of the Fourth International. Political isolation on the one hand, the revolutionary masses on the other, were the algebraic forces which would pressure into action the incipient revolutionary forces inside Russia. But the revolutionary forces, by force or fraud, were captured by Stalinism. It is at this point that the world conception split open. It is just here that the whole world picture is different from what Trotsky envisaged and has profoundly affected all mankind and the fortunes of the Fourth International.

Trotsky believed that the traditional national bourgeoisies could still offer a cushion of super-profits to Stalinism. Here are his own words:

> Ten years ago it was predicted that the theory of socialism in one country must inevitably lead to the growth of nationalist tendencies in the sections of the Comintern. This prediction has become an obvious fact. But until recently, the chauvinism of the French, British, Belgian, Czechoslovak, American and other communist parties seemed to be, and to a certain extent, was, a refracted image of the interests of Soviet diplomacy ('the defense of the U.S.S.R.'). Today, we can predict with assurance the inception of a new stage. The growth of imperialist antagonisms, the obvious proximity of the war danger and the equally obvious isolation of the U.S.S.R. must unavoidably strengthen the **centrifugal nationalist tendencies** within the Comintern. Each one of its sections will begin to evolve a patriotic policy on its own account. Stalin has reconciled the communist parties of imperialist democracies with their national bourgeoisies. This stage has now been passed. The Bonapartist procurer has played his role. Henceforth the communo-chauvinists will have to worry about their own hides, whose interests by no means always coincide with the 'defense of the U.S.S.R.' ....
>
> Fifteen years of uninterrupted purges, degradation and corruption have brought the bureaucracy of the ex-Comintern

4 It has a long and deeply instructive history.

> to such a degree of demoralization that it has become able and anxious to openly take into its hands the banner of social-patriotism...
>
> The ruling Moscow clique will reap the just fruits of fifteen years' prostitution of the Comintern. ("A Fresh Lesson," *New International*, Dec. 1938, pp. 363–4.)

It was possible to make Trotsky's mistake in 1940. No one seriously challenged the strictly economic analysis on which he based his expectations. But what is one to say of a writer in 1947, who with the whole experience, the hard facts of Stalinism between 1940 and 1947 behind him, proceeds to make it again and then puts this forward as Trotskyism?

The Repudiation of the National State

It is clear that we face a serious problem. It is not to be solved by analysis of "bureaucracies" but by analysis of capital.

The economic program of the Fascist party of Germany will teach us much. The program was not the expansion of finance-capital in the classic manner but the integration of whole economies, all their capital and all their labor, into one solid continental bloc to serve the interests of capital accumulation, political mobilization, strategic attack and defense. How organic to the contemporary world is this movement to break the old national chains is proved by the example of Italy, the ally, and France, the enemy of Nazism. In the last stage Italian Fascism became the direct agent of German capital in Italy. Petain and Laval who had long dreamt of a coordinated French and German capital hesitated before and during 1940, but immediately after the June defeat recognized the historic process.

This is the bourgeois movement. What Trotsky failed to see, but what we have no excuse for failing to see, is that such is the disintegration of capitalism, that the proletarian parties even though counter-revolutionary, can no longer pay allegiance to the old national boundaries. Capitalism had neither economic basis nor ideology nor future to win the Stalinist leaderships and the Stalinist cadres to national allegiance. But breaking with the national state and all the phenomena of capitalism and unable to turn to the "latent socialism" in the masses as Lenin did in 1917, they held tightly to another pole of power, the Stalinist state and the Red Army.

The Stalinist parties do not aim at independent Stalinist states. They do not, as the pre-1914 Shachtman likes to think, aim, at doing for themselves in France what the Russian Communist Party had done in 1917. The Stalinists understand the movement of the centralization of capital. In France and Italy they aim at the incorporation of these countries as satellites with greater or lesser freedom into one coordinated European syndicate. They may be forced to do otherwise but that is their aim.

"All democracy," says Lenin, "like every superstructure in general (which is inevitable until classes have been abolished, until classless society has been created) in the last analysis serves production and in the last analysis is determined by the production relations prevailing in a given society." [*Selected Works*, Vol. IX, p. 52] Now that European fascism is destroyed, Stalinism in various stages of development is the organic political superstructure of the day. Irrespective of the will and consciousness of men it serves or seeks to serve production. But it is capitalist production, which at the present stage can live only by the suppression of those millions whose very joining of the Communist Party but partially expresses their proletarian determination to remove themselves forevermore from wage slavery which is precisely what Stalinism has in store for them. The concept of abolishing wage slavery would transform Stalinism into a revolutionary organization depending on mass force. That they cannot unloose without destroying themselves. They are therefore balanced between the fundamental antagonisms of the capital–labor relation on a razor's edge, combining the extreme development of capital – already slipping from the hands of the bourgeoisie – and the proletariat, also slipping out of the clutches of the bourgeoisie.

Stalinism – the Agent of State-Capital

Engels would have recognized Stalinism at once. In his personal supplement to *Socialism, Utopian and Scientific*, he wrote:

> Partial recognition of the social character of the productive forces forced upon the capitalists themselves. Taking over the great

> institutions for production and communication first by joint-stock companies, later on by trusts, then by the State.

The political agency of this last is Stalinism and it will do it with or without the bourgeoisie but so far always with the Red Army.

> The bourgeoisie is demonstrated to be a superfluous class. All its social functions are now performed by salaried employees.

But Engels did not end there. He continues:

> Proletarian Revolution – Solution of the contradiction. *(note that, Comrade Germain, and note what follows.)* The proletariat seizes the public power, and by means of this transforms the socialized means of production, slipping from the hands of the bourgeoisie, into public property. By this act, the proletariat frees the means of production from the character of capital they have thus far borne, and gives their socialized character complete freedom to work itself out. Socialized production upon a predetermined plan becomes henceforth possible.

The leadership and policies of the Communist Parties therefore can be summed up as the political form corresponding to the final form of capitalism, state capitalism, which involves, not the expansion of finance-capital in the old way, but the incorporation of individual economies within powerful centralized economies operating on a continental scale. These parties are as organically related to capitalism in this stage of its development as was the Second International to the classic finance-capitalism of Lenin.

We understand these parties best by realizing that **even if Stalinist Russia had never existed and the proletarian revolution had been delayed, some such political formation as the Stalinist parties would have appeared**.

The Stalinist leaderships are a further stage of development of Menshevism in 1917. The Mensheviks trembled before the "anarchy" of the revolutionary fervor of the masses and fear of the inevitable intervention. The Stalinist leaders in France and Italy tremble before the same phenomena infinitely multiplied. Historically, in appearance, subjectively, they support the Kremlin and therefore they oppose the proletarian revolution. But Marx never tired of pointing out how often the appearance of things contradicted their essence. The logical analysis of the Stalinists is the exact opposite of the appearance, i.e., their historical origin and subjective motivation. It is because they despaired of, fear and oppose the tremendous leap in the dark of the proletarian revolution that they attach themselves like leeches to the tangible power of the Kremlin.

Germain, enclosed in the theory of power, prestige and revenues for the Stalinist bureaucracy in France, just as he is enclosed in the theory of power, prestige and revenues in Russia, cannot grasp the fundamental movement.

It is the class struggle which is decisive for the policy of Stalinism. If the irreparable bankruptcy of capital drives the Stalinist leadership to break with the national state and look to an established power, **it is the driving force of the mass movement which keeps them there**. It is only where there is a comparatively feeble mass support that the subjective decision is theirs. But with the violent rejection by the masses of bourgeois society and the complete bankruptcy of the national state and the national economy, the Stalinist leadership, unable to turn to the masses, must look elsewhere. They are held to the Kremlin by as tight a social bond as held the reformists to the bourgeoisie. They are terrorized first by the revolutionary masses and only afterwards by the G.P.U.

The Petty-Bourgeoisie, Not the Kremlin

Imprisoned in his analysis of the Stalinist bureaucracy, Germain does not understand the corruption of the Stalinist parties. It is only superficially a Stalinist bureaucratic corruption. It is a class corruption, corruption by the petty-bourgeoisie.

In *Left-Wing Communism*, Lenin, analyzing the international significance of the Russian Revolution, insisted that an exact analysis in each country of the position of the petty-bourgeoisie between the bourgeoisie and the proletariat was decisive for the clarification of revolutionary politics. In the early years the petty-bourgeoisie had contributed substantially to the parliamentary corruption of the Second International.

The Stalinists use the petty-bourgeoisie who turn to it to corrupt the proletariat. These petty-bourgeois elements, revolutionized, are ready to expropriate the national bourgeoisie, and "plan the economy." But their conception of planning is the administration by themselves of the productive forces, including the proletariat. The prejudices and fears of intermediate classes have been used by frightened leaders in every revolution to corrupt and demoralize the vanguard and strengthen the rearguard against it. Nothing but the revolutionary movement of the proletarian masses will draw the petty-bourgeoisie to it, genuinely revolutionize it and leave thousands of bureaucrats without a medium for corruption.

Thus, while not in any way minimizing the subjective features of the Stalinist bureaucracies in France or Italy and the origin of their practices, we must first show that their corruption is fundamentally bourgeois, based upon bourgeois fears, a bourgeois economic solution of economic problems and a bourgeois response to the acute class relations in the country.

The Errors of Munis and Germain

Once the contradiction between the proletarian and the bourgeois content of the Stalinist Parties is grasped, political policy flows from it. If it was necessary to raise the slogan of the Social-Democracy to power, then with all the more urgency it is necessary to raise the slogan of the Communist Party to power. But Stalinism has already shown that it will strip capital of every covering, including private property, in order to maintain wage-labor, the proletariat as proletariat, the fundamental condition of capitalist slavery. Absolutely unable to make the leap that Lenin made in 1917, it is therefore compelled in its own right to become even more deeply the quintessential expression of capitalist barbarism. In the closest inter-penetration with this slogan therefore must be posed the complete reorganization of society, Soviets, factory committees, preparation for the seizure of power, tearing to pieces of the old social order, and abolition of the bourgeois state, abolition of the bourgeois army, arming of all the able-bodied population, workers' control of production, peoples' courts. So acute are the contradictions of capitalist society that the slogan without the program concretely presented for the full revolutionary transformation of society is a betrayal of the masses. The revolutionary program without the slogan is a denial of that mobilization for the social overturn which the Communist Parties represent.

At a later stage the masses may create other organizations of their own, Soviets or nation-wide anti-Stalinist factory committees. When they do, a new situation arises. But the very social character of the Stalinist parties and the objective acuteness of the social relations creates the possibilities of vast organized splits in that party, impossible in the old days when these partly were merely political parties. It is the presence of a revolutionary program and not mere agitation about wages which can accelerate, clarify and solidify these.

The contradiction contained in the very term critical support becomes altered by the objective conditions. The support becomes merely a basis for the criticism, the merciless exposure of Stalinism and the revolutionary release of the masses which alone can overcome it.

Munis confuses the Stalinist parties in Western Europe with the Stalinist parties in Eastern Europe. He opposes the slogan of the Communist Party to power in France because, according to him, the Stalinist Parties immediately set out to destroy the power of the proletariat. The destruction of the self-acting organs of the proletariat is a matter of the relationship of forces, national and international, at a given moment. In 1917, the Bolshevik Party first supported the slogan of the Soviets to power; then came to the conclusion that the Soviets had gone completely over to the government, and decided that the revolution would have to be made against the Soviets; and finally, came to the conclusion that this judgment was mistaken and returned to the policy of making the revolution through the Soviets. A Bolshevik party that cannot in theory apply this revolutionary flexibility will be swamped in the always violent oscillations of the revolutionary struggle for power. Any policy based upon the conception that Stalinism can at will destroy the revolutionary proletariat, is a denial of the premises of the proletarian revolution itself. Munis' policy is to be entirely rejected.

Munis takes it for granted that the Communist Party in power will automatically mean the destruction of the proletariat and repudiates the slogan for Western Europe as well as for Eastern. But Germain who attacks Munis sticks to the slogan in Eastern Europe where the Communist Party is not only the organizer of a bourgeois police-state but is the unashamed agent of a foreign power. Worse still, Germain has now begun to analyze "the level of consciousness" and of "organization" of the proletariat in a manner which, if he were taken seriously, would make his use of the slogan a suicidal adventure. How can he correct Munis? Shachtman hopes for a good long "democratic interlude" where everyone would be able to talk the matter out democratically.

The International should stop and ponder what this means. It is not differences of views but lack of clarity which causes confusion. It is lack of a firm guiding line from the leadership, the majority, around which differing tendencies can align themselves, that generates centrifugal tendencies. The responsibility for this lies entirely on Germain and those who think like him. And none of the crimes of Shachtman should prevent Germain being brought to book for the superficiality and falseness of his analysis of the Stalinist parties.

E. THE NATURE OF THE PARTY 1947

The self-mobilization of the masses is the dominating social and political feature of our age. Now that we see it in sufficiently concrete manifestation, it is possible to link these manifestations to the recent historical past and draw strategic conclusions for the future.

The old divisions between the economic management of production, the social leadership of society, and the political party-traditional in the bourgeois national state and reflection of the capitalistic division of labor, are doomed. The classes recognize the need for a new social organization and the response is the modern party. Yesterday the national state used the party. Today, to meet the changes, internal and external, the party uses the national state.

Hitler in 1930 declared:

> I replace the simulacrum of bourgeois patriotism by the national solidarity of my party and the simulacrum of Marxian socialism by the social justice of the same party. While parliamentary Germany falls in ruins, a new Germany is being born.

He recognized the modern political party as a new social formation, and his efforts as an expression of it. The genius of Lenin, nourished by the needs of Russia, anticipated as a conscious organized activity, what is now turning out to be the necessity of the social structure.

Such tremendous social expressions can only arise from profound economic changes and needs, which are concentrated in the statification of modern production. As the Johnson-Forest tendency stated in its Resolution on the International Situation (April 27, 1946):

> **THE STATIFICATION OF PRODUCTION**
>
> In France and Britain any movement of the masses brings them immediately into direct conflict with their own leaders as rulers or direct representatives of the government. The simplest of immediate demands concerning the high cost of living, of the right to strike become questions of state policy and continually pose before the workers the fundamental question of state power. Thus, the social structure of state power in statified production places the workers in a situation where any determined struggle compels them to face the problem of creating their own organization in order to bring pressure upon, and if necessary, to break the power of the labor leadership as virtual functionaries of the existing government.
>
> **Statification and Bourgeois Democracy**
>
> The struggle for democracy, particularly in the advanced countries, is no longer the struggle for the extension of popular rights....
>
> **Statification of Production – The Ideological Struggle**
>
> Today, when the proletariat says democracy, it means above all, not bourgeois democracy... Its social concepts are dominated by the idea that the catastrophes of modern society are caused by the private ownership of the means of production. The necessity that these be taken away from the monopolists and be returned to the nation to be planned for the good of all has now achieved the 'fixity of a popular prejudice.' This is one of the greatest advances ever made by human consciousness both in its implicit rejection of the concept of class distinction and in the scores of millions who hold it.

Driven by the economic and social transformations (and the psychological responses engendered by these), the oppressed classes turn away from the old political forms and seek to encompass the need of the all-embracing statified production by an all-embracing organization.

History is and will be inexhaustible in its combinations. Soviets and the mass party may appear together or in combined forms. The new content constantly appears in old forms. According to Trotsky, it was not until the Bolsheviks had to dissolve the Constituent Assembly *in 1918* that the concept of proletarian democracy became clear to Lenin. But the proletariat and the petty-bourgeoisie have already shown enough to warn us that, despite the inevitable defeats, advances and retreats, we are in a new stage of mass mobilization.

In the light of the above, all the proponents of the theory of the backwardness of the modern proletariat show nothing but their backwardness. They are completely incapable of analyzing the actions of the proletariat as revolutionary manifestations of the present stage of the capital–labor relation, i.e., statification of production. For petty-bourgeoisie and proletariat the modern party is not a political party for voting. It is a social organization for action – a response to objective and psychological needs. The American proletariat may not form a party at all until it feels the need for creating a party of this kind. It will be political only in the formal sense but its appearance will signify a readiness to break the old society entirely to pieces. It is not only Shachtman who does not understand this. Germain preaches an abstract revolutionism, attacks Shachtman with a lot of words, and then in July, 1947, informs us that the post-war proletariat started "from a much lower level of consciousness and organization than that of 1918." This is monstrously false, a direct reversal of the objective truth, and the result of complete misunderstanding of the Marxist method.

The origin of this retrogression is the same as Shachtman's. Germain sees the proletariat too much from above, in its relation to the Stalinist parties and not sufficiently in its response to the capital–labor relation. And this (also like Shachtman) he practices because his basic theoretical conceptions are governed by the theory of the degenerated Workers State and all that this implies. The theory of the degenerated Workers State implies the theory of the degenerated workers. But never by one comma did Trotsky govern his general analysis by concepts of this kind, and we shall pursue it wherever it appears. Germain's "Trotskyism" is his own misconception and misappropriation of certain of Trotsky's ideas, and the application of them in a manner and in spheres alien to Bolshevik analysis.

The New Parties and the Old Slogans

From this concept of the proletariat we can draw certain political conclusions:

1) We can see in a new light the full significance of Trotsky's audacious use of the propaganda and agitation *for the formation* of a Labor Party in the United States. With the tremendous self-mobilization of the masses which he anticipated, he infused the slogan with the full revolutionary content, **exactly the same procedure that Lenin followed in his advocacy of the Constituent Assembly during 1917**. The driving mass movement, if it were powerful enough, would in action slough off the reformist shell of the slogan, aided as always by the quite unacademic education of the counter-revolution. This was Trotsky's conception of the Labor Party slogan. The principle acquires a burning actuality. The "consciousness" of the masses today is no guide to the revolutionary violence of their explosion tomorrow and still less a guide to the millions who rush to create the new social formations. Slogans like National Liberation, the Constituent Assembly, and nationalization of industry (a slogan repudiated by the Third Congress) acquire the same, no less and no more, significance than the Labor Party slogan in the United States.

2) With a clear conception of what the revolutionary masses mean by a party the whole conception of the role of the Bolshevik Party, i.e., of the Fourth International in the concrete circumstances, does not narrow but expands. The rise of the mass movement raises with it the role of the Bolshevik Party. Every Bolshevik becomes what Trotsky warned in 1940 that he – not merely the apparatus – must become, an officer in the proletarian army. The theoretical range, the practical political capacity, the revolutionary dynamism, the discipline, the cohesion, are needed not so much to meet the offensive of the bourgeoisie, as was the fate of a party based upon the small Russian proletariat. It is needed to meet the offensive of the proletariat. Subjective and objective move towards fusion. Every revolutionary unit of "the subjective factor" becomes an objective unit for the revolutionary preparation and then as a rallying center for scores and perhaps hundreds of proletarians on the road to proletarian democracy.

This is the problem in Britain. The Labor Party is a party of the old kind. It is strangling the new British proletariat. The advanced workers therefore either break out in sudden wildcat strikes or face the government in impotent but implacable hostility. At a certain stage the proletariat will transform or fuse, but somehow totally reorganize in the modern sense its organizations to meet the needs and satisfy the desires for which the present Labor Party and the unions are totally unfitted. To stimulate, observe and develop this and nothing else but this is the main task of the revolutionary vanguard in Britain. But to carry out this policy demands a clear conception of the origin and destiny of the social movement of the proletariat which is developing before our eyes.

3) At this stage of statification, says Engels, the proletariat seizes the public power. These mass rushes to the party are the form whereby the proletariat girds itself to seize the public power and thereby begin the withering away of the state. But the defense of the statified production against the proletariat involves a similar mass mobilization or organization. The Communist Party of Russia is such a mass mobilization. In its completed form it is not a proletarian party at all. In it the razor-sharp capital–labor contradiction that exists between the proletariat and the Stalinist leaderships inside the parties of Western Europe has been resolved entirely at the expense of the proletariat and in favor of state-capital. The motive force of the Communist Parties in Western Europe is the attack on capital. The motive force of the Communist Party of Russia is the defense of capital in its present form – state-capital. Thus they are exact opposites. For Germain and Shachtman this organic distinction does not exist because they have continually evaded answering even to themselves what Engels meant by state-capitalism.

CHAPTER II
State Capitalism

> In the trusts, freedom of competition changes into its very opposite – into monopoly; and the production! without any definite plan of capitalist society capitulates to the production upon a definite plan of the invading .socialist society.
> – F. Engels, *Socialism, Scientific and Utopian*

A. THE REVOLUTION THIRTY YEARS AFTER

The state in State and Revolution is the state of state-capitalism. In 1923, Lenin, near the end of his working life, could say: "Whenever I wrote about the New Economic Policy I always quoted the article on state-capitalism which I wrote in 1918." In the article referred to (note the date, 1918) Lenin said categorically that from petty-bourgeois capitalism "it is one and the same road that leads...to large-scale state-capitalism and to socialism, through one and the same intermediary station called 'national accounting and control of production and distribution.' Those who fail to understand this are committing an unpardonable mistake in economics." In 1916 Lenin in *Imperialism*, a popular outline, did not go beyond plain monopoly capitalism. He was careful to point out the difficulties of capitalist planning by trusts. By

1917, he noted in many places the rapid acceleration to state-capitalism and in State and Revolution he modified his conception of planning. By October he moved still further and declared that the imperialist state could organise production "according to a general plan."

Trotsky, under the influence of the Russian experience, attacked the idea of national accounting and control by the capitalist state. In the few pages devoted to state-capitalism in *The Revolution Betrayed*, he was careful, however, to leave the theoretical possibility open. But Trotsky at any rate did not live to see contemporary Poland, Yugoslavia and Czechoslovakia. The old argument used to be that there was a qualitative difference between the most advanced statification by the bourgeoisie and the state property of Russia achieved and achievable only by social revolution. The argument used to be that because of the antagonisms of private ownership, the capitalists could not plan. But today in Eastern Europe all the basic industries are in the hands of the state. Germain now gives a motley variety of ridiculous reasons why planning will be impossible in Yugoslavia, Czechoslovakia and Poland. They are already a mill-stone around his neck. For Yugoslavia has published its plan and it is modeled on the blueprint of Stalin.

Behind all the evasions of all that Marx, Engels and Lenin said on state-capitalism, behind the evasions of the Yugoslavian reality, so humiliating to contemplate, is hidden a desperate fear that should the bourgeoisie or, **for the sake of argument**, any other agency, hold all the capital in its hands, then it would be possible to "raise the level of the productive forces." Then the proletariat would not be the gravedigger of capitalism. Then Marxism would be Utopia. It is in this theoretical graveyard that the bureaucratic collectivists dance their witches' dance.

The Proletariat as Economic Force

The history of Stalinist Russia has demonstrated in life that the only solution to the basic antagonism of capitalism, on which rest all other antagonisms, is the emancipation of labor. The proletariat is the greatest of all productive forces. It is its creative power which alone can raise the productivity of labor and establish society on new foundations. It is precisely the necessity to suppress this un-paralleled economic force which is the basis of totalitarianism.

Germain will not listen to us – then maybe he will listen to this:

> Democracy is a form of state… at a certain stage in the development of democracy, it first rallies the proletariat as a revolutionary class against capitalism, and gives it the opportunity to crush, to smash to atoms, to wipe off the face of the earth the bourgeois, even the republican bourgeois, state machine, the standing army, the police and bureaucracy; to substitute for all this a more democratic, but still a state machine in the shape of the armed masses of workers who become transformed into a universal people's militia.
>
> Here 'quantity is transformed into quality': **such** a degree of democracy is connected with overstepping the boundaries of bourgeois society, with the beginning of its socialist reconstruction. If, indeed, all take part in the administration of the state, capitalism cannot retain its hold. The development of capitalism, in turn, itself creates the **prerequisites** that **enable** indeed 'all' to take part in the administration of the state. Some of these prerequisites are: universal literacy, already achieved in most of the advanced capitalist countries, then the 'training and disciplining' of millions of workers by the huge, complex and socialised apparatus of the post-office, the rail-ways, the big factories, large-scale commerce, banking, etc., etc. (*Selected Works*, Vol. VII, p. 91.)

We hope, but we doubt very much, that this is clear to you, Comrade Germain. The universal literacy, the training, disciplining, etc., **these are the new economic forces**. Do you doubt it ? Then read on.

> With such economic prerequisites it is quite possible, immediately, overnight, after the overthrow of the capitalists and bureaucrats, to supersede them in the **control** of production and distribution, in the work of **keeping account** of labour and its products by the armed workers, by the whole of the armed population.

All the emphases are Lenin's. Is it any wonder that Germain here takes refuge in an impenetrable silence, a silence as deep as his silence on the state-capitalism of Engels? Here is Lenin again.

> To elucidate the question still more, let us first of all take the most concrete example of state-capitalism. Everybody knows what

> this example is. It is Germany. Here we have 'the last word' in modern large-scale capitalist technique and planned organisation, subordinated to Junker-bourgeois imperialism. Cross out the words in italics, and, in place of the militarist, Junker-bourgeois imperialist state, put a state, but of a different social type, of a different class content – a Soviet, that is, a proletarian state, and you will have the sum total of the conditions necessary for socialism. (*Selected Works*, Vol. VII. pp. 364–5.)

Lenin saw to the last inch the class and human difference in production by the bourgeois revolution and by the proletarian revolution.

> The positive, or creative work of organising the new society was carried out by the property-owning bourgeois minority of the population. And the latter carried out this task relatively easily, not-withstanding the resistance of the workers and the poorest peasants not only because the resistance of the masses that were exploited by capital was then extremely weak owing to their scattered character and ignorance, but also because the fundamental organising force of anarchically-constructed capitalist society is the spontaneously expanding national and international market.

Today the workers are no longer ignorant. The world-market is in chaos. What must be substituted?

> In every socialist revolution – and consequently in the socialist revolution in Russia which we started on November 7 (October 25), 1917 – the principal task of the proletariat, and of the poorest peasantry which it leads, is the positive or creative work of setting up an extremely intricate and subtle system of new organisational relationships extending to the planned production and distribution of the goods required for the existence of tens of millions of people. Such a revolution can be successfully carried out only if the majority of the population, and primarily the majority of the toilers, display independent historical creative spirit. (*Selected Works*, Vol. VII).

Ethics or Economics

Note the words "intricate and subtle system of new organisational relationships." The proletariat and the proletariat alone can reorganize the social relations of labor. The average American worker laughs at the boasted efficiency of American production. Once his mental subordination is destroyed, he can point out means and ways of increasing the productivity of labor which are impossible in the relation between exploited, hounded, degraded, antagonistic labor and the oppressive and merciless supervision which is capital.

Not in Marx's theories but in life, this, with its superstructural relations, is the problem of the day, and with it mankind comes of age. Germain in 1947 fears that the transformation of private property into state-property, with the situation of the worker unchanged, is a solution to the economic problems of society. It is this that blinds him to the full significance of the revolutionary mass movement that has been developing under his eyes. He cannot meet it, analyze it, understand it and help it to understand itself. The workers control of production is the only emancipation of labor, the only reorganization of society on a new productive basis. History will record that nowhere was this **idea** fought more bitterly than in the revolution vanguard itself. And this it did because it had to defend – God help us! – the revolutionary aspects of Stalin's dual-charactered bureaucracy, not in 1940 but in 1947.

B. THE STATE THIRTY YEARS AFTER

Rut if the revolution has thus matured thirty years after 1917, so has the counter-revolution. The achievement of state-capitalism is at the same time the beginning of the disintegration of capitalism as a social system, and today we can watch the process at all stages of development. We have a perfect and concrete example of it in Stalinist Russia. Our analysis of Stalinist Russia, including the victory in or around 1936 of the counter-revolution over the proletarian state in Russia, can be found elsewhere.[5] Here we are concerned with the theoretical conclusions for world development as a whole which must be drawn from the experience of Russia.

---

5 Internal Bulletin of the Workers Party, March 1941; Resolution on the Russian Question, October 1941; "Russia – A Fascist State," *New International*, April, 1941; "Russia, and Marxism," *New International*, Sept. 1941; "An Analysis of Russian Economy," *New International*, Dec. 1942, Jan. 1943, Feb. 1943; "The Nature of Russian Economy," *New International*, Dec. 1946, Jan. 1947; "After Ten Years – a review of Trotsky's Revolution Betrayed," *New International*, Oct. 1946.

In the early stages of capitalism, the objective movement, i.e., the expansion of surplus value, and the desire for profit on the part of the capitalists, the phenomenal expression of this objective movement, coincide. The capitalists therefore, have a subjective interest in the system. The power of private capitalists over the social conditions of production and the power of capital as a general social power are one and the same thing. This is what is known as private or free enterprise. And the system can work because it finds in it a class of human beings, individuals who freely represent it. They take the lead in the struggle for social progress, the extension of their own democratic rights and even the democratic rights of the population as a whole.

With the increasing development of capitalism, however, the law of value undergoes violent and incessant revolutions. A discovery like atomic energy alters the value composition of capital and throws disorder into all economies.

> To the extent that such revolutions in value become acute and frequent, the automatic nature of self-developing value makes itself felt with the force of elementary powers against the foresight and calculations of the individual capitalist, the course of normal production becomes subject to abnormal speculation, and the existence of the individual capitals is endangered. These periodical revolutions in value, therefore, prove that which they are alleged to refute, namely, the independent nature of value in the form of capital and its increasing independence in the course of its development. (*Capital*, Vol. II, p. 120.)

Capital, as state-capital, is the exact reverse of planned. It is independent as never before and runs riot. The dominating force of society becomes the objective movement of the self-expansion of capital which crushes everything that stands in its way. Which capitalists or bureaucrats can control this? Russia shows anew that these are, as Marx and Engels continually pointed out, the target of its destructive malevolence. It destroys them.

> The contradiction between capital as a general social power and as a power of private capitalists over the social conditions of production develops into an ever more irreconcilable clash, which

> implies the dissolution of these relations and the elaboration of the conditions of production into universal, common, social conditions. (*Capital*, Vol. III, p. 310.)

The capitalist is only the personification of capital, and not only small capitalists but all capitalists lose all right to existence before the sway of capital as this strange, independent, elemental social power. In reality, it is the nature of capital itself to destroy capitalists. It throws out small capitalists, then one group of capitalists (the Jews) then wipes away practically a whole capitalist class as in Germany, tears whole sections of them out of Poland, Yugoslavia, Czechoslovakia. The terror of capital against the capitalists is only exceeded by its terror against labor. Its highest peak is the incessant purges among the rulers of Russia themselves. To continue to believe that this is not due to production relations is to make these men masters of their own fate and inhuman monsters. [Sooner or later this question will arise.]

The terror is rooted in the relations of production and the need to control workers. When the workers reach the stage that they are today, then the relations of production demand a terror which spreads through all society. It is because of this, and not because of the wickedness of the Stalinists and the Nazis, that the modern barbarism is the most barbarous history has ever seen. It is suppression of the democracy of the modern masses, the mightiest of economic and social forces, which compels totalitarian savagery.

Idealism, Not Historical Materialism

Trotsky gave the motive power of the economy as the "prestige, power and revenues" of the bureaucracy. This is wrong in theory and practice. How do you measure prestige and power in economic terms? The proportionate revenues of the bureaucracy are no more and in all probability are much less than the revenues of any other ruling class.

Within the categories of Marxian political economy, if is the machinery, the industrial plant, its need for constant expansion, its rapid obsolescence and renewal in the competition on the world-market – it is this (c – constant capital) that dominates both the wages (v – variable capital) and the surplus (s – surplus value). Not man but capital rules. How is it possible for Marxists today not to see that in

Russia it is the drive for constant expansion, the drive of capital for self-expansion, the competition with United States capital, the need to renew capital according to the law of value; how is it possible not to see that this is the economic driving force of Stalinist economy and not prestige, power and revenues? Today every politician and economist governs himself by this.

The refusal to recognize this is beginning to stifle our movement. Germain[6] must say that social relations of production in Russia are superior to the productive relations of capitalism. This means "the will and intelligence" of men are no longer subordinated to the objective movement of production. They have risen superior to it. That is what is meant by the capacity of the bureaucracy to plan.

But this supposed advance, this first step into the realm of freedom, has resulted in the most horrible, the most degrading, the most monstrous tyranny mankind has ever known, and worst of all, a tyranny that competes for world power, is now in Berlin and aims at the Atlantic. As long as Germain persists in limiting its crimes to the sphere of consumption, he has to continue to say that the bureaucracy plans badly, it cheats, it distributes unequally. Its human capacities and human sensibilities become social agencies. This is not even vulgar, far less historical materialism. It has a long history both in philosophy and political economy. It is idealism. Even before Marx, Hegel recognized this mode of thought and its political consequences.

The Johnson-Forest tendency made this precise characterization of Trotsky's position on Russia in 1941. Now in 1947, as we see the results of false theory in our movement, we reaffirm our positions. For us, production in Russia is subject to the laws of the capitalist world-market. The bureaucracy is as subjected to the basic laws of capitalism as is any capitalist class. All the monstrosities of the Stalinist society are rooted in the laws of the capital–labor relation which reach their highest expression in Russia. If not, then the road is open to subjectivism, the interchanging of the dialectical role of party and masses, exaggeration of the power of Stalinism in Russia and in Western Europe; inability to base theory undeviatingly on the objective move-

6 The absurdities of Germain's political economy in regard to Russia, the crudities of his underconsumptionism cannot detain us here. See Appendix.

ment of the proletariat. From end to end our movement in varying but substantial degrees, the process is at work. The theoretical remedy is to kill it at the primal root – the production relations in the factories of Russia.

Terror for Workers and for Rulers

> The authority assumed by the capitalist by his personification of capital in the direct process of production, the social function performed by him in his capacity as a manager and ruler of production, is essentially different from the authority exercised upon the basis of production by means of slaves, serfs, etc.

Modern social authority is the slave of capital.

> Upon the basis of capitalist production, the social character of their production impresses itself upon the mass of direct producers as a strictly regulating authority and as a social mechanism of the labor process graduated into a complete hierarchy. This authority is vested in its bearers only as a personification of the requirements of labor standing above the laborer. It is not vested in them in their capacity as political or theoretical rulers, in the way that it used to be under former modes of production. (*Capital*, Vol. III, p. 207).

For a period the capitalistic authority appears to be separate from the political, which intervenes only periodically, at first to help in the release of constricting forces (reform and revolution) and later by counter-revolution to discipline the always growing revolt of the proletariat, the revolt against the suppression of what capitalism itself creates. In its latest stages capital as a regulating authority of the labor process and particularly of socialized labor, must bring the state and all social relations and manifestations directly under its control. But the contradiction between the capitalistic productive forces and the social relations are not destroyed, they cannot even be suppressed in the developed stages of state-capitalism. They are now no longer inherent, existing in essence. They take on reality, they appear. The antagonistic social relations, **relations between people**, in Russia are not suppressed. The relation becomes the actual daily struggle of the active antagonism driving to its resolution, perpetual revolution and counter-revolution. The *modus vivendi* of the economy can only be political counter-revolution – the **daily** purges, the daily destruction and corruption of workers, workers organizations, and of managers. This is the national existence. The political struggle assumes the form of the ruthless antagonism of production. At a certain stage, the traditional functions and organizations of the state, army, judiciary, administration cannot serve their purpose. Power rests in the secret police, Gestapo or N.K.V.D. The industrial reserve army assumes the form of political prisoners. Political prisoners become the form of the industrial reserve army. Capital which, in Marx's words, came into the world dripping blood and dirt, now functions only in blood. And as this barbarism spreads its shadow over Europe and Asia, and driven by its own logic, reaches its tentacles out to the proletariat of the world, Germain continues to repeat that this is the regime transitional to socialism, that nationalized property is progressive, and that this quintessence of social tyranny has its root in the struggle of men over the distribution of food and clothing. Thus, his analysis of Stalinist Russia today is the direct repudiation of what Marx struggled all his life to establish: the objective basis in production relations of all the subjective manifestations of human evil.

Under state-capitalism, the Russian bureaucracy is no "dual-charactered" hybrid, product of its revolutionary origins and capitalist destination. It is the naked counter-revolution. Trotsky's analysis is that the growth of the bureaucracy and the power of the Stalinist state are due to the struggle over consumption, that the Stalinist state is organized nine-tenths for stealing, that the coming revolution is not a social but a political revolution. All this cannot stand repetition today. The Stalinist state is organized on the basis of capitalist production in the epoch of state-capitalism. The revolution will be profoundly social – an **economic** revolution, the release of economic forces, the creative and productive forces of the proletariat.

C. THE COMMUNIST PARTIES OF RUSSIA AND EASTERN EUROPE

The analysis of the economy defines the ruling party. The Russian Communist Party exists on the backs of the defeated proletariat. But the proletariat in Russia contains within itself the same explosive qualities as the proletariat in Western civilization, subjectively more so because of the experience of three revolutions. The main purpose of the party, therefore, is to keep the proletariat subjected to the process of capitalist production.

But such a process is not achieved overnight. It was achieved and is maintained in Russia by the bloodiest, the most savage, and the most cold-blooded counter-revolution in history. And it is this which explains the role of the Communist Parties in Eastern Europe. They are the creatures of the Red Army and the economic, political and diplomatic power, and discipline and training of Stalinist Russia. It is under the protection of the Kremlin and the Red Army that they are seeking to complete as fast as they can and with whatever allies they can put their hands on, the transformation that has already taken place in Russia.

These are colonial regimes. Not in an article but in a decree written on the day after the revolution in October, Lenin defined the colonial regime:

> If any nation whatsoever is forcibly retained within the boundaries of a given state, if, in spite of its expressed desire – no matter whether that desire is expressed in the press, at popular meetings, in party decisions, or in protests and revolts against national oppression – it is not permitted the right to decide the forms of its state existence by a free vote, taken after the complete evacuation of the troops of the incorporating or, generally, of the stronger nation, without the least pressure being brought to bear upon it, such incorporation is annexation, i.e., seizure and coercion. (*Selected Works*, Vol. VI, pp. 401–2.)

When a Marxist is unable to accept this and cannot apply it to regimes like Poland, Yugoslavia and Hungary, then it is time, Comrade Germain, for him to stop arguing with his opponents and re-examine his own premises.

The Polish individuals who rule Poland and administer its laws and direct its armies are not Poles at all. They are as Russian as the Kremlin, tied to it not only by training, fear, and the solidarity of crime, but by the far deeper recognition that within society as they see it they must be vassals of Russian or Anglo-American imperialism. Their allegiance is not subjectively to the Kremlin but objectively to the centralized capital of Russian state-capitalism.

Let Germain deny this and add yet another to the coils of steel-wire in which he is assiduously entangling himself. Any support of the Communist Parties as they are is a betrayal. They play and must play the same role as the Communist Party of Russia, with the added burden of a colonial dependence as necessary to them as it is to the imperialist power.

CHAPTER III
Imperialism Thirty Years After

A. "VAST STATE-CAPITALIST AND MILITARY TRUSTS AND SYNDICATES"

The imperialism of state-capitalism is the key to the understanding of the present stage of imperialism all over the world and the concrete forms of its development. Lenin, writing in the heat of a similar, but less developed, type of world disintegration was able to give us a wonderful Marxist forecast of just the contemporary developments.

> Marxists have never forgotten that violence will be an inevitable accompaniment of the collapse of capitalism on its full scale and of the birth of a socialist society. And this violence will cover a historical period, a whole era of wars of the most varied kinds – imperialist wars, civil wars within the country, the interweaving of the former with the latter, national wars, the emancipation of the nationalities crushed by the imperialists and by various combinations of imperialist powers which will inevitably form various alliances with each other in the era of vast state-capitalist and military trusts and syndicates. This is an era of tremendous collapses, of wholesale military decisions of a violent nature, of crises. It has already begun, we see it clearly – it is only the beginning. (*Selected Works*, Vol. VII, pp. 315–6.)

What Lenin described in 1918 was the beginning of barbarism. Today we are thirty years further. The whole world is caught into the **imperialist** conflict. There are only two divisions.

If Stalinist Russia is a vast state-capitalist and military trust, American imperialism is a vast state-capitalist and military syndicate, and the distinction is evidence of the clear vision with which Lenin saw into the future.

B. AMERICAN IMPERIALISM

During the war the United States government transformed itself into a mighty state-trust. It planned its production and consumption. But the American state-trust, in the struggle for world domination, embarked upon a government-regulated world-economic program. It integrated with its own the economy of Great Britain; it poured billions into the thin economic veins of its allies; and it bought and distributed agricultural production on a world-wide scale. It acted as collective capitalist on a hitherto undreamt-of scale.

With the end of the war approaching, Russia, through the Stalinist parties, backed by the Red Army, operated directly in the proletariat. The United States operated through the Social Democracy and the bourgeoisie, backed by the American army and American economic power. But the joint unity was against the proletariat only. The United States now carries on open preparation for war against its rival. From end to end of the world its economic power economically supports the most reactionary and oppressive regimes, at the head of which list stands the Chiang-Kai-Shek regime in China. America supplies arms and economic resources to aid France in the suppression of Viet Nam, and the Dutch in the suppression of Indonesia. It supports the reactionary regimes of Turkey, Iran and Greece and even the Fascist Franco. It maintains the tottering capitalistic regime in Japan. It is the support and ally of every counterrevolutionary regime in Latin-America. It shares equally with Russia the major guilt in the drawing and quartering of Germany. The State Department becomes the virtual dispenser of billions of dollars of foreign trade. The latest venture is the proposed "Marshall Plan" – a gigantic scheme to reconstruct the shattered economy of Western Europe, and by this means to control its economy and politics completely as an outpost of American trade and a bastion against both Stalinist Russia and the proletarian revolution.

By its enormous, swollen bureaucratic expenditures at home, its war preparation, direct and indirect, its control of the World Bank and all international economic agencies, the State Department's manipulations of foreign trade and foreign loans, and the American government has become the economic arbiter of billions of productive forces and hundreds of millions of people. Only an economist fetishism can fail to see that in its struggle with Russian capital for world domination, the American state acts as the center of a vast state-capitalist syndicate within which it dominates the economics and politics of its subordinate allies. These stick to it for the same reasons that their counterparts stick to Stalinist Russia, terror of the proletarian revolution and fear of a rival imperialism.

But great as is the economic power of American imperialism, this is counter-balanced by the colossal drain upon its resources of maintaining the world-wide system of satellites within its syndicate, the hatred it engenders in revolutionary forces everywhere, and the revolutionary instincts, strivings and industrial organization of the American proletariat, the greatest social force the world has ever known. Not in any ultimate historic but in the immediate sense, American capital faces the same catastrophic violent destruction at the hands of the proletariat as does Stalinist Russia.

It is only when we have this as our basis that we can analyze the disintegration of relations between nations and the concrete forms of the tasks history now imposes upon the classes.

We must understand the background of Lenin's mind when he made his priceless formulations.

C. THE INTERWEAVING OF IMPERIALIST, CIVIL AND NATIONAL WARS

Lenin in 1916 made a triple division of the countries of the world. Division I was the countries of Western Europe and America where the progressiveness of bourgeois national movements was at an end. Division II comprised the countries of Eastern Europe including Russia. There the bourgeois national movements for national liberation were on the order of the day. In Division III were India, China, and other colonial countries where the bourgeois national movements were just beginning. Those divisions, the result of geographical conditions and social relations, are equally valid today, with, however, tremendous changes which involve the new relations and new tactical approaches to the struggle for socialism.

In 1947, Division I, after thirty years of capitalist disintegration, shows that the bourgeois-national movements are no longer merely "not progressive." **They have abandoned their historic roles. The bourgeoisie of France, Italy, Germany, and Japan no longer believes in national independence.**

It is therefore natural that among the advanced countries this movement to the syndicate is most powerful. The syndicate alone is suited to the advanced countries of Western Europe.

As soon as we look at Lenin's Division II we can see an entirely different structural form. Russia was an oppressor nation in 1916 but 1917 showed that even its own bourgeois problems were dependent upon the proletariat for solution. The history of Russia to date shows that even the Russian proletariat, in isolation, has proved incapable of solving not only the socialist problems, but even the democratic problem of self-determination. Hence Trotsky in 1939 raised the slogan of an independent Ukraine. The whole history of Russia since 1917 and the miserable, bloody history of the countries of Eastern Europe since 1916 have shown, as we would expect, that there is no salvation for them as capitalist countries. But long before 1947 it was possible to see that there is no salvation for them at all as isolated countries, capitalist or socialist. Estonia, Latvia, Lithuania, Czechoslovakia, the Ukraine, the Balkan countries, Greece, and Poland, **cannot survive even as isolated socialist states**. Germain's Marxism does not know what every Polish workman knows. For nearly two hundred years a bourgeois Poland was constantly partitioned and repartitioned. The Poland of 1918 was an artificial creation, maintained by a balance of power which was destroyed in the war. Now today Poland as an isolated nation, capitalist or socialist, is finished forever, and the same is true of the other countries of Eastern Central Europe.

Germain calls them "the buffer-countries." His pro-Stalinism, the spectacles through which he views relations between nations as between classes, has led him to endorse a title which is the exact opposite of the truth. Buffer is precisely what they cannot be. Their whole history shows that they have to **belong**. After 1848, Hungary and later Czechoslovakia, clustered around Austria (hence the Dual Monarchy) in order to save themselves from a greater oppression – Tsarist Russia. After 1918 some of them formed the Little Entente, under the economic and political guidance of France. The decline of France swept them into the orbit and then the domination of Germany. It is no accident that at the first shock Germany wiped away the Polish and Yugoslav bourgeoisie. The defeat of Germany swept them into the power of Russia. The conclusion is obvious. It is that for Austria, Yugoslavia, Czechoslovakia, Greece and the others, any economic organisation which is not based on the Socialist United States of Europe or at the very least on a Federation of Socialist States in Eastern Europe is reactionary.

As national units they are doomed either to participation in a socialist federation or subordination to a vast state-capitalist trust or syndicate. This is the given stage of the given epoch, the result of the centralization of capital. This is the economic and social movement growing steadily through the decades which has now reached a climax in the coalescence around the state-capitalist military trust of Russia. The concrete movement might have been otherwise but it is only a theory which can explain it. Lenin did not join the terms, State, capital, military and trust by accident. The competition on the world-market fuses these into one centralized force. Politics becomes the most highly concentrated and comprehensive expression of the laws of the world-market. Germain, in the face of the reality, continues to divide the economic from the strategic needs of a totalitarian state.

Today in Europe as far south as Greece, but above all in Poland, there is and can be no isolated civil war. Every conference, every economic deal, all loans, "relief," peace-settlements, production, grabs of territory, withdrawal or maintenance of troops, and elections, are governed by the struggle for the domination of Europe between the United States and Russia. All political opposites, national and international, politics and economics, peace and war, are beginning to assume identity. In 1940 the small states, pawns in the hands of the big ones, only had freedom to a limited extent, to choose between their masters. Today Germany, the heart of Europe, has no freedom of choice. In the cabinets of France and Italy the rival powers have their representatives evenly matched, and every step is calculated for its effect on the world proletariat and the struggle for power between a state-capitalist military trust and a state-capitalist military syndicate.

CHAPTER IV
Poland – Where All Roads Meet

There is no better example than Poland itself of how a national situation develops, how Marxist policy changes, and how we must concretely apply Marxist fundamentals. In dealing with Poland and self-determination in 1903, Lenin poses two epochs – (1) the epoch of the formation of national states ending about 1871 and (2) the epoch of 1903, "the age of desperate reaction, of extreme tension of all forces on the eve of the proletarian revolution..."[7] During both periods, Poland was divided between Germany, Austria-Hungary and Russia. Yet the policy for each period was sharply distinct. In the first period Marx and Engels raised the slogan of self-determination for an independent bourgeois Poland to help defend democratic Europe against Tsarist reaction. In the second period Franz Mehring denounced this policy. The Polish Socialist Party, the P.P.S., was gaining ground among the petty-bourgeoisie with its slogans of armed insurrection and terrorism against Tsarism. It sought to unite the three parts of Poland into a bourgeois state. By 1902, said Mehring, an independent bourgeois Poland is impossible and therefore the Polish proletariat in all three sections should fight "unreservedly" with its class brothers. Lenin, cautious as

7 Lenin lived perpetually with these ideas, even in 1903.

always, stated that he would not declare the impossibility of a bourgeois Poland as categorically as did Mehring. But he agreed sufficiently for the time with the analysis to accept the political conclusion as absolutely correct. The unity of the proletariat of the oppressed and oppressing nations, a cardinal point in the Leninist doctrine of self-determination, here assumed an extreme form.

Yet long before 1916 the specific historical circumstances, alliances, relations, etc. which culminated in the war of 1914 had opened up new possibilities for an independent bourgeois Poland. Lenin said so plainly and now defended the right of self-determination for a bourgeois Poland against Tsarist Russia. His main reason now was that the right of self-determination did not and could not under capitalism mean freedom from an economic domination by great powers. Such freedom was impossible under capitalism. But the right of self-determination meant political freedom of a state, **freedom for the full and free development of the class struggle, freedom for the proletariat to develop its democratic instincts and tendencies**. Further, the slogan of self-determination had undergone a class development. The Russian liberal bourgeoisie had hitherto supported the slogan, but under the blows of the Russian proletariat, they became antagonistic to it. Thus Bolshevism took over the slogan as a proletarian demand.

This at once involves the important distinction between the right of self-determination and the raising of the demand.

So tentative and conditioned is the actual demand as distinct from the abstract right, that Lenin, while defending the right of Norway to secede from Sweden, states that if such a demand could result in a European war, then while the right should be fought for, the demand should not be raised. That is for the Shachtmanites to think over. On the other hand, Lenin, in 1916, quotes Engels to the effect that colonial India would be justified in making a revolution against "victorious socialism" in Britain. And this is for Germain and his co-thinkers to ponder over.

A Stage Beyond 1916

The Johnson-Forest Tendency, in its strategy and tactics on the question of self-determination, has never at any time lost sight of the relation between the given stage of the epoch, the particular type of country involved, and the given stage of class relations; and the effect of this demand in Europe, for instance, upon the struggle for the common goal, the Socialist United States of Europe.

In 1943, immediately after Stalingrad, which outlined the future course of bourgeois Europe, the Johnson-Forest Tendency, in violent opposition to the Shachtmanite thesis on the national question, pointed out that henceforth there could be no independent bourgeois states of Estonia, Latvia, and Lithuania.

In 1946, this time against the I.K.D., we poured as much scorn as we could on their idea of "autonomous," "bourgeois states" as preliminary to socialism. We said:

> During World War I it was one of Lenin's basic arguments on self-determination that economic domination did not mean political domination. Today, and that is the new stage, economic and political domination go hand in hand. ("Historical Retrogression or Socialist Revolution," *New International*, Jan., Feb., 1946.)

This was a tremendous step forward from Lenin's position. By May 1946 our analysis of the stage of the epoch had been in our view sufficiently confirmed by the concrete happenings in Europe. In our international resolution therefore we elaborated policy.

> The Anglo-American bourgeoisie and the Second International seek to bribe the proletariat to accept the overlordship of American imperialism in return for bourgeois-democratic forms and American economic aid.
>
> Russian imperialism and its Stalinist satellites seek to tyrannize and then to bribe the proletariat to accept the virtual overlordship of Russian imperialism under the guise of the European continent in a new social order...
>
> Under these circumstances it is a matter of life and death for the Fourth International to oppose both these ruinous roads, and it can do so only by linking the struggle for national economic rehabilitation to the struggle for the Socialist United States of Europe.
>
> A Socialist France in a Socialist United States of Europe
>
> A Socialist Poland in a Socialist United States of Europe

> A Socialist Germany in a Socialist United States of Europe.

From this basic analysis we then outlined a concrete policy for Russian dominated Europe and Asia:

> In Eastern Europe the proletariat faces the colossal task of overthrowing not the delegated but the direct military power of the Russian state. In its rear, it has the armed forces of Russia occupying Germany. Under these circumstances, the movement against Russian domination in the separate countries must therefore orient towards the unification of proletarian struggle in the directly oppressed states, including Germany. A mass revolutionary movement with a common program and an advanced social goal has the best possibility of shaking the discipline of the Russian armies and re-awakening in them the traditions of the October Revolution.
>
> With this perspective the proletariat is assisted in the carrying out of the daily struggles against the oppressing imperialist power. Without a perspective of international struggle, the advanced workers will be less fortified against Stalinist propaganda or the defeatism which will await intervention on the part of another imperialist power as the only means of ridding itself of the Russian domination, exploitation and plunder.
>
> A similar situation in Eastern Asia (Korea, Manchuria, etc.) poses similar tasks for the Fourth International.

We have never wavered. Ours is a political position, rooted in the most careful, systematic analysis of the developing relations between the classes and the nations within the struggle for the world of two vast state-capitalist trusts and syndicates.

Now today it is possible to summarize our position even mere concretely and bring to bear upon it our whole analysis:

1. Class rule over the proletariat in Poland is impossible without active support from an outside imperialist power.

2. Poland cannot be ruled by the Polish proletariat as long as the present balance of power continues.

3. Far more than Mehring and Lenin in 1903, it is necessary to see that the Polish proletariat must orient itself first and foremost towards

its class brothers. The objective situation demands that same repudiation of both sides which Trotsky envisaged in Spain in 1938 in case the intervention on both sides assumed dominance. The politics of Poland is the politics of war.

4. This exemplifies the form taken in our day of the perpetual Marxist struggle for the unity of the proletariat. In Marx's day it was a struggle to integrate the economic and political aspects. We have traced it and shown that today, objectively, as a result of the concrete conditions of decaying capitalism and the concretely developing and invading socialist society, revolutionary policy must unite the proletariat internationally for the solution of immediate needs.

Shachtman and Bourgeois Politics

Examination of the policies of Shachtman and Germain shows the confusion into which they fall because neither has taken the trouble to establish a sound theoretical basis.

Shachtman begins by declaring the complete independence of the revolutionary party. Thereby he is ready to show that the revolutionary party is for everything revolutionary, including the Socialist United States of the World. Having, as he believes, covered himself up from all "attacks" (literary squabblings and debating points) he then gets down to business. His policy is the policy of "critical support to Mickolajczk." Now critical support of Mickolajczk can mean only one thing – that Shachtman is for the victory of Mickolajczk, not for all time, but as a first stage. This policy is bourgeois politics, pure and simple. To say that Poland will be free under Mickolajczk is a fantasy. Mickolajczk stands or falls by Anglo-American imperialism. It is necessary to remind this realistic practicalist of a little realism. Stalin in Central Europe is not playing games or making debating points in pre-convention discussions. Today he is holding Poland – the gateway to Germany.

Furthermore, with Russian troops in Germany, to open out a serious struggle in Poland under the leadership and with the prospect of victory to Mickolajczk is to invite at once the complete military occupation of Poland by Russia, and as far as human reason can judge, to take the responsibility of pushing the world towards world war. It is possible for a revolutionary party to advocate this. But it is obvious that Shachtman writes his little articles and scores his little points, devoid of any serious consideration of what his policies imply.

Germain and Bourgeois Economics

Some of this, more or less, Germain sees and points out with devastating effect. But what is Germain's own policy? Germain advocates critical support of the Beirut regime. He sees and calculates boldly on the inevitable intervention which alone can make Mickolajczk a serious contender for power. He is politically blind to the actual concrete intervention which alone makes Beirut able to hold the power. Isn't this shameful? Germain does not say as a serious Trotskyist might say: "In this situation, control of Poland is needed to defend the precious 'planned economy' of Russia. Therefore we repudiate self-determination and declare that the Polish workers must for the time being defend the regime in the interests of the degenerated but proletarian state." He does not say: "This Polish economy is the economy of a workers' state, and is or can be, transitional to socialism. Therefore it must be defended." Instead he denounces the regime as bourgeois and declares that the nationalizations are qualitatively the same type as those of France or Britain. He knows, he must know, that these bourgeois nationalizations are defended and maintained by the power of a foreign oppressing power which makes Poland a pawn of its economic and political plans for the domination of Europe and Asia. He knows, he says later, that the Polish proletariat faces the, mortal enemy of its own self-determination. The political decisions about the Polish regime are made in Moscow. The contending parties travel there and lay the case before Stalin who tells them what to do. And yet he says that this regime must be critically supported. In reality he is objectively committing an unpardonable deception. He is defending Stalinist Russia but does not dare to face it.

The price is already being paid and a bitter price it is. Germain now subscribes to the completely petty-bourgeois conception that it is the Beirut regime which defends the Polish proletariat and its supposed conquests from Mickolajczk. As well say that British imperialism defended the democratic rights of Britain against Hitlerism.

In reality it is not the attacks of Mickolajzck which compel Russian domination. It is the Russian domination of Poland which gives such strength as he has to the attacks of Mickolajczk. For years the Polish proletariat has been under a systematic terror from Stalinism as the preliminary to the domination of Poland. Russia's first step in Poland was to hand over the Warsaw proletariat to the Nazis. If Russian troops were withdrawn even today, the Polish proletariat and the masses would be able to take care of Mickolajczk. It is to misunderstand completely the history of Eastern Europe to believe that it is Russian troops which prevent the victory of the Fascists. The Fascist? would be as helpless as in Greece. A genuine proletarian uprising in Poland would find Mickolajczk ready to come to terms with Beirut **as he has already tried to do and as many in his party are doing now**. We are of course under no illusions about any withdrawals in Europe by any occupying power. But it is something entirely new in our movement to call the **bourgeois police state** the defender of the proletariat and its "gains."

Shachtman Meets Germain

The price Germain pays extends from his own theories and Poland to the rest of Europe. Germain (and here he is at one with Shachtman) has not a single word to say about the burning question of the relation to the proletariat of Europe, to begin with, Germany. It is beyond credibility. What preoccupies all other participants and observers gets not a single word from Germain.

Not only is the relation of Poland to Western Europe general. It is particular. What is to happen to Eastern Germany which is now Western Poland? The Germans have been driven out. Millions of Poles are installed. Do Germain and Shachtman propose to accept this? Are they for "restoration" to Germany? Then they will drive out or tenderly lead out the Poles? Are they for the old boundaries or the new ones? The bourgeoisie and the Stalinists recognise that the old Europe is gone. They are creating a new one in their own image. The people too know that the old world is gone. The powers hold millions of Germans. Benes transfers millions of Sudeten Germans. The Jews fight their war into Palestine. Stalin has transferred practically the whole populations of Estonia, Latvia and Lithuania. In the French Zone there are communities of Germans ready to accept French citizenship. Millions of Germans may become French citizens, and welcome ones, tomorrow.

Vast numbers of Europeans are ready to emigrate, so violent is the revulsion against the old society. Still more significant. After the war, all the power of Stalin's police was unable to stem the tide of the great migration back to Western Russia from war work in Siberia. With the first serious breakdown in military discipline we shall probably see tremendous mass migrations and re-transferences **initiated by the whole peoples themselves**.

Ten per cent of Russian soldiers in the occupying armies desert. That is a warning, a warning that at a new stage the masses, by fraternization among themselves can break the discipline of Stalin's army.

Today, the revolutionary movement should issue slogans and appeals for fraternization among the peoples. The Fourth International should take the lead in stimulating and holding before Poles in Western Poland and Germany everywhere the concept of a fraternal mingling of peoples aiming in time at a mass, a revolutionary disregard of the bourgeois national boundaries. The scales of bourgeois violence and barbarism can be matched only by revolutionary violence on a corresponding scale.

Germain finds that Shachtman's slogan of the "free Republic" is a substitute of "empty and abstract slogans reflecting petty-bourgeois and bourgeois nationalist ideology" instead of the immediate struggle for material interests. But what does Germain substitute instead? He substitutes the slogan of an "Independent Soviet Poland." If Shachtman's free Republic is an abstraction there are no words to express the ethereal character of the struggle Germain outlines for a Soviet Poland.

> The duty of Polish revolutionists is to **explain patiently** to the masses that Stalinism constitutes the antithesis of Leninism; that the struggle for the socialist revolution means the struggle for a **workers democracy**, a genuine **Soviet democracy**; that the activities of the Stalinist emissaries are a condemnation of the Soviet bureaucracy but not of the Communist ideal which the latter extirpate in Russia itself in rivers of blood; that the Bolshevik-Leninists are resolute partisans of the right of peoples to self-determination; that consequently the central slogan

> around which they must mobilize is that of an INDEPENDENT SOVIET POLAND, which would differentiate us as much from the conservative bourgeoisie as from the degenerate bureaucracy. (*Fourth International*, Feb. 1947.)

"Patiently explain." Is this reference recognized? Of course it is. This is what Lenin told the Russian Bolsheviks to do in 1917 when the workers had in essence political power but believed in the Soviet. This is what Trotsky preached to the Russian workers against the usurpations of the Stalinist regime in a deformed workers state. Germain equates the bourgeois nationalization and the police regime with the Soviet and the democratic self-mobilization of the masses in Russia before October. From the idealization of nationalization in Stalinist Russia comes this idealization of bourgeois nationalization in Stalinist Poland. Show us a single line of Trotsky to justify this monstrosity as Trotskyism.

Germain says that the Shachtmanite thesis and the thesis of the Fourth International show their differences best on the Kielce program. They do. Shachtman is supporting critically Mickolajczk's camp which participated in the pogroms. And Germain? He says that "if the armed struggle between the militia and the illegal bands had been drawn out...there can be no doubt we would have called upon the workers of Kielce to mobilize on their own." (our emphasis). This is indeed a revelation. Is this too Trotsky's policy? The Transitional Program says that at every conceivable opportunity the workers should **form their own guards for their own defence**. But for Germain, Beirut's police-state is a stage to the Soviet regime. This too he has deduced from the theory of the degenerated workers state. Germain's Trotskyism therefore now tells the Polish workers to wait and see how "their" regime protects them from Fascism before intervening.

From Opportunism to Anarchism

Germain's position pursues him everywhere, driving him to right and left. Shachtman proposes that the Trieste workers vote to join the Italian bourgeois democracy. Germain denounces him and wins one of his usual easy victories. But Germain must have a position. He dare not tell the Trieste workers to join Tito's state. He says himself that this would mean "the bureaucratic strangling of the workers movement." Opportunism now makes its plunge into anarchism. Germain comes out for "A Soviet Commune in Trieste." This, even if it lasted "for only a few weeks" would, we are told, act as a magnet to the advanced masses of the countries occupied by the U.S.S.R. and give a powerful impetus to the class struggle in Italy. And this piece of romantic desperation goes unrebuked in our movement.

In reality, today, the Fourth Internationalists in Trieste should warn the Trieste workers against such suicidal nationalistic action. They should ruthlessly in their policy denounce the national boundaries and preach day in and day out the unification and coordination of the Trieste working class movement primarily with the Italian proletariat. They should denounce both the Italian democracy and the Tito police-state as agents in the strangulation and destruction of Europe. They should strive to inculcate the necessity for united, coordinated action with the program, concretely worked out, of a socialist federation. The Trieste workers should be taught to look upon themselves as a part of the proletariat of Southern Europe. They have the right of self-determination but that right is historically and politically conditioned. They should be told that this right exercised for and by themselves means economic and political ruin. Imagine a 1947 Marxist advocating a nationalized economy for Trieste! If Germain cannot see the town of Trieste as a part of the international proletarian struggle, how can he see Poland? The Trieste workers may be **compelled** to fight a battle for power in Trieste. Every stroke of policy should show that they have been forced into this, and do not see it as any program of their own. And the **only** way to prevent this action being forced upon them is to make them understand and struggle for the mass intervention (mass strikes, demonstrations) of the Italian proletariat on their behalf at the slightest sign of pressure. They should be taught that their own actions should be theoretically and organizationally linked to the actions of the Italian proletariat and the resistance to Tito. This is not only sound Bolshevism. It is exactly the type of policy which the workers in Southeastern Europe followed in the last stages of the war. The Soviet Commune of Trieste should be driven out of our movement. The property not being nationalized, the workers are therefore advised to die gloriously "pour encourager les autres."

Germain on one side (and Shachtman on the other), cannot recognize that the slogan of the Socialist United States of Europe is the only practical, concrete basis of revolutionary policy. In the specific forms of their errors they complement their joint refusal to see international socialism as the solution, not tomorrow, but today. Germain is violent against Anglo-American intervention. Shachtman is violent against Russian intervention. Neither can say "We denounce both interventions." Neither can see the European proletariat as the basis of proletarian strategy today. Neither understands what is meant by making the Socialist United States of Europe the unifying slogan of revolutionary policy in Europe. They remain theoretically within the national boundaries of Poland when all participants in the struggle, even the Polish workers, recognize that the struggle is international. Shachtman, swinging in the air, can only hope in vain for "bourgeois political democracy." Germain falls back on the bourgeois nationalizations. The policy we advocated in May 1946 has corresponded exactly to the actions of the most advanced of the Polish workers. They saw the "civil war" for what it was and held aloof from it. In Cracow the proletariat voted neither for Mickolajczk nor for Beirut. An independent Socialist Party has been formed supporting neither side. But this policy is supposed to be a policy of abstentionism.

So when Hitler attacked Czechoslovakia in 1938 and the Austrian workers said "Down with Hitler! Not for Schusnnigg," this was presumably an abstention. When Trotsky said that you could not abstract Hitler's attack on Czechoslovakia from the whole complex of modern Europe and told the workers to oppose both, this too becomes abstention. And today when we refuse to abstract Poland from a milieu in which is concentrated the fundamental conflicts of world politics, and draw policy to suit, this too becomes abstention.

We have other allies than Mickolajczk to struggle for and with. We have to win over the soldiers of the oppressing power – Russia.

The Russian soldiers will see Mickolajczk as the vanguard of Anglo-American imperialism. In Germany all the defeated classes and fascistic elements will rally to the support of Mickolajczk. Within the Russian Army itself, all the Kravchenkos, those who see salvation for Russia in bourgeois democracy, these are the defeatists who will he pulled over to the side of Mickolajczk. The genuinely proletarian elements of the Russian army can be won over neither by Beirut nor Mickolajczk. They must see the European proletariat. This is 1947.

And the German proletarian vanguard? Does Germain believe that they will demonstrate, make a general strike, initiate political activity for the victory of Beirut? This will mean nothing more than the tightening of their own noose. And the victory of Mickolajczk? For the German workers it means only the further entrenchment of Anglo-American imperialism. The German workers want a destruction of both imperialisms. The Russian workers want the destruction of both. The Polish workers need the same. Hence in case of a civil war in Poland the revolutionary vanguard in the army of Beirut will have a defeatist policy. It will see to it that its representatives in Mickolajczk's army do the same. It declares in advance: a plague on both your houses. The proletariat will carry on mass demonstrations against this pseudo-civil war: But if the war does come, it does not abstain. It does not shun the war. It holds on to what arms it can get and struggles to create against both Mickolajczk and Beirut an army for a socialist Poland, freed from both Anglo-American imperialism and Russian, and reaching out to Russian soldiers, the German proletariat, and all the other proletariats oppressed by Russian imperialism. It does not precipitate such a struggle. It works patiently to build its cadres. It bitterly opposes being forced into war. But if the war should come this is the policy it will carry out.

Shachtman will say with elaborate sarcasm: The Johnson-Forest position is based on the "Cannonite" conception that the war is still going on. For occupied Europe it is. Imperialist armed occupation of a country is a state of war. Joint occupation of one country and of a whole continent is a state of war. But there is more to this.

The 1944 Theses of the Fourth International (*Fourth International*, March 1945) referred to the "integration of military actions of service to the U.S.S.R. within the framework of a general working-class offensive." Does Germain propose to prepare the German proletariat and the French proletariat today for this tomorrow? Or does he actually propose to draw this to its conclusion, if the Red Army marched on France? Is this too Trotsky's position? Where and when will this stop? Day after day during the last two years we stand more and more bewildered before this question: What advantage, what single advantage does Germain gain for the proletariat by this defense of the U.S.S.R. in return for the monumental confusions and burdens which it places upon the Fourth International and the working class?

CHAPTER V

Parties, Tendencies And Programs in the Fourth International

From the concrete exposition of policy in one of the most difficult and therefore most revealing problems in the modern struggle for socialism, it is necessary now to pass to the political tendencies in the Fourth International. But here also the terms sectarian, Menshevik, Economist, Bolshevik, make no sense except in strict relation to the analysis of the mass movement.

A. SECTARIANISM TODAY

How difficult and misleading it is to use these words like sectarian unless within the framework of an analysis of the epoch is demonstrated by the example of Munis. In 1944 Munis and Peralta put forward the following program for the European workers; and in 1946 repeated it in another publication.

> 1. The arming of the proletariat must be extended to the entire proletarian class and to the poor peasants. At the same time, we must demand the disarmament and dissolution of the armed forces of the bourgeoisie (army, police, etc.) and achieve this as soon as the occasion presents itself....
>
> 2. ...The nationalization of industry, of finance capital or of the

> land by the capitalist state must not deceive the masses. That will be a trick of bourgeois, Stalinist and reformist coalitions to preserve capitalist property. Any confiscated property must not be delivered to the bourgeois state. The proletariat must administer the economy by itself and establish a single plan for all countries to the degree that international contact among the exploited permits this. It is already possible to elaborate a project of unified production between the French, Italian and Belgian proletariat; tomorrow it will be possible with the German, Spanish, Greek, and Russian workers, etc. Although the coalitions between bourgeois, Stalinists and "socialists" supported by the bayonets of Wall Street, of the City and of the Kremlin prevent for the moment the putting into practice of a social plan for Europe, the project ought to be established and defended by the revolutionaries of every country. In the face of the reactionary designs of the governmental coalitions, it would be an enormous force for propaganda, of persuasion, and of socialist agitation.
>
> 3. ...Where...committees do not exist, the immediate objective of the masses ought to be their establishment. Where they exist, they must be united on a national scale by the means of the Congress of Committees which will study and resolve the problems of the masses and of the social revolution. The committees, of workers peasants and soldiers of different nationalities ought to make contact on the first occasion possible and create a Supreme Council of European Committees.... What precedes can be summed up in this slogan. All political power to the Committees of Workers, Peasants and Soldiers and, for The masses in general: Socialist United States of Europe. (LE GROUPE ESPAGNOL OF THE 4TH INTERNATIONAL IN MEXICO, Manifesto of October 31, 1944, translated from the French.)

We need not subscribe to every word. But the conception is magnificently concrete. Munis also makes it perfectly clear that a lull in the offensive of the proletariat does not alter the validity of this program. As we shall show, in this he is absolutely correct. There is not an ounce of sectarianism in this and people who in one place preach the approaching downfall of civilization and then reject as sectarian a program for the international mobilization of the proletariat are playing with revolution.

Yet Munis is a sectarian. His sectarianism consists essentially in his rejection of the slogan, the Communist Party to power. We unceasingly propagate the committees and the international plan, but until we have the committees, the Stalinist parties represent a profound mass mobilization and must be supported as we have described. The question is: What does Munis represent?

In 1920 during the revolutionary turmoil after the last war the Communist International faced the disease of infantile leftism, at the bottom of which was a refusal to make a revolutionary use of bourgeois parliaments. This sectarianism had its origin in the failure of the revolution because of the corruption of the Social-Democracy by bourgeois parliamentarism.

Munis represents the infantile leftism of today. Where bourgeois parliamentarism corrupted the proletariat in the period that culminated in the foundation of the Third International, the developed objective situation has produced a new type of betrayal, the betrayal of the Social-Democracy and Communist Parties with actual state power in their hands. Just as the left in 1919 reacted too violently against the corruption that had preceded them, so Munis reacts against the corruption that has preceded the historic opportunities presented to the Fourth International.

Germain, who is able to explain little, cannot explain Munis. He therefore cannot prepare the Fourth International for what can be a very serious danger: the violent reaction of increasing layers of the revolutionary masses as they see through Stalinism and their refusal to recognize the necessity of tactical compromises with even the bureaucracies of the Communist Parties in Western Europe.

But with Munis, his political positions carry over into his organizational practices. The same un-Bolshevik ferocity that he displays to the labor leadership – not Stalinism alone – he displays in regard to the leadership of the Fourth International.

Munis represents a tendency which has emancipated itself from the preoccupation with Stalinism as a mode of thought. His attack is on the labor bureaucracies, both Stalinist and reformist. His basis is obviously the proletarian revolution, the mass movement, as we have outlined it in this pamphlet. It is far different with the other tendencies.

B. MENSHEVISM TODAY

The Johnson-Forest tendency in 1946, analyzed "the dual heritage" in the position left by Trotsky to the Fourth International: on the one hand, the Leninist program for the mobilization of the proletariat for the world proletarian revolution; on the other, the Russian position. We pointed out further that the movement was dividing along two lines – not on mere defeatism, but on the Russian experience in relation to the world revolution.

Now it is becoming perfectly clear that the political tendencies in the International are dividing along the lines we have indicated. The I.K.D., in its theory of historical retrogression, has elaborated the most fully and drawn to its ultimate conclusion those theories which are rooted in the degeneration of the Russian revolution.

The theory of retrogression claims that the degeneration of bourgeois society brings with it the degeneration of the proletariat. This has received its most finished and revealing manifestation in a passage from a thesis submitted to the 1946 Convention by the I.K.D. Fighting to break through the wall of conservatism of the W. P. Majority, the Johnson-Forest tendency had challenged it with the statement that in the United States no one could exclude the possibility that within two years a general strike could take place and the workers could form, if not Soviets, workers' councils. The W. P. Majority which in a few months (such is centrism) would go much further than this, not in theory but concretely, professed to see in this a forecast of the last stages of the insurrection and the struggle for power. The I.K.D., however, took up the challenge directly and produced the following. The quotation is long but it has the advantage of saying everything.

The I.K.D. on Socialism

> The necessity for a revolutionary leadership is recognized in words, but one has not the least notion how it has to be constituted. In order to convince ourselves of this let us push the insanity to extremes and assume that J. R. Johnson takes power with his party in the spring of 1948. Of course, Johnson will have Soviets all

over and have at his command any number of different kinds of 'workers' committees.' In addition the party will be imbued with the kind of wisdom which Johnson takes for 'Marxism.' We assume further that even the mass of workers have understood Johnson 'fully and completely.' Then what?

On the basis of the 'conception' of the party which especially Johnson and the official Fourth hold, we would then experience a catastrophe of unimaginable extent.

We would be faced by this problem: Army and industry national and international politics, agriculture and trade, imports and exports, educational system and propaganda, scientific research and technical apparatus, statistics and medicine, administration, housing, and a hundred other branches would not only have to be re-organized, but also **controlled** and **led**. We would find ourselves in a **concrete** situation facing Stalinism as well as the church, the reformists, the other parties, the international diplomacy and the armed counter-revolution. Finance, regulation of currency, legislation, postal service, radio, motion pictures, psychology, philosophy, pedagogy, literature, art, family life, sports, recreation, penology, and a thousand other questions would create troubles which Johnson's book-learning does not dream of. Faced with all these difficulties which (let us repeat emphatically) cannot be enumerated and are of gigantic dimensions, Johnson would realize that he has not understood "Das Kapital" if for no other reason than that he doesn't understand anything about bourgeois society. Where enormous knowledge and utmost many-sidedness are required he would operate with a dead schemata. He would be at the mercy of the bourgeois specialists in every detail, for better or for worse.

Does anyone imagine that one could do without this army of specialists or **force** them to cooperate through the 'dictatorship' because there are sufficient numbers of technically trained workers to keep production running? But just to maintain production and distribution, economists, architects, technicians, engineers, physicists, chemists, experts in forestry, mining, transportation, agriculture, etc., are needed without end. All these people would not let themselves be **commandeered** by a party which is not in

> a position to **check up on them**. Under such circumstances even large stratas of workers would assume definite traits of a "ruling" class in the bad sense and fall prey to this ever-present danger, the easier the more ignorant the party, and thus bring the workers to power as pure products of the capitalist environment. The workers then would have practically no more to offer than their "proletarian" self-conceit or the arrogance of their 'historical' mission. They would commit stupidity after stupidity. They would be forced to rule by naked power, arouse all the world against themselves and lengthen the chain of difficulties from this unforeseen point to the final decline of the revolution.
>
> In civilized countries the conquest and the maintaining of power are much more difficult than in backward ones (for example, in barbaric Russia). The more developed a country the more knowledge is required, and the more difficult is it to convince the specialists, to win them over, and to discipline them. If Johnson, trusting in the development of the class struggle, would, after taking power, assemble them and submit his 'plans' they would remark to each other after the first address: Why, this is a prattler! He thinks he can solve difficult questions with agitational speeches.'
>
> Of course, every great revolution makes a great number of scholars, specialists, and intellectuals of all kinds willing to join and be at its disposal. Only it has to be a **great** revolution and not a Johnsonnade upon which one will look with a superior smile or with panic as upon a folly, a childishness, a queer idea or an insane adventure. In the absence of a party which has already gained great political and moral authority the achievement of socialism will be lost every time." ("The Crisis of Socialism and How to Overcome It," BULLETIN OF THE W.P., Vol. I, No. 17, pp. 16–17.)

The strictly political implications of this are of profound importance for the clarification of our movement and the understanding of the class struggle. The extract shows that the state-capitalism of the I.K.D. is merely another name for bureaucratic collectivism or the managerial society of Burnham. The technicians and the managers will defeat the most powerful proletariat in the world in the most advanced society in the world because of the absence, not of a party, but of a special type of party. So special is this type of party that of necessity there looms the probability of "a third alternative." It is not only the seizure of power that is feared. It is what happens after.

This party obviously is not a party consisting predominantly of workers. It is a party able to handle the fearsome hub of problems detailed by the I.K.D., a party of the educated elite. This is in theory the class basis of the Stalinist corruption of the proletariat in Western Europe. Thus the I.K.D. represents not Menshevik tendencies in general. It is a Menshevik tendency which corresponds to the degeneration of the Third International as classic Menshevism corresponded to the degeneration of the Second. Because Germain is unable to analyze the proletariat and the Stalinist parties, he is thereby as unable to analyze the I.K.D. as he is baffled by Munis.

The practical consequences of the policy of the I.K.D. are no less important. **All who hold these views are and must be mortal enemies of the revolutionary struggle for power and the revolutionary propaganda and agitation which go with it. These must wait for the party. Agitation for revolution, propaganda for revolution, is pushing the proletariat to its certain destruction. The proletariat is not ready. The party is not ready.**

From this flows the unbridled, the ungovernable ferocity and rage with which the extreme representatives of this tendency attack the Fourth International, the bitterness and hate with which they review the whole past history of the proletariat, and the platonic construction which they call the role of the party.

As always in the historical manifestations of a logical line, the supporters of the I.K.D. show every variety of deviation and combination of contradictory phenomena, usually an empirical response to national conditions. But all through run certain conceptions, e.g., the backwardness of the masses, and the predilection for a realistic, "practical," and "non-sectarian" policy, in other words, the drowning of Bolshevism in ill-concealed Menshevik politics. They show a fanatical interest in statistics of boom and economic "stabilization." The maintenance of some sort of equilibrium by an American financed recovery is vital for these tendencies. Without it the struggle might be precipitated by the backward proletariat upon the unready party. In varying degrees the policy is the policy of "the lesser evil," i.e, the labor status quo, until such time as the proletariat and the party are ready. For them always the status quo. In the U. S. they capitulate to American petty-bourgeois radicalism and the union bureaucracy; in Britain they capitulate to the labor government; in France they capitulate to the Stalinist bureaucracy. For a second it might appear that the French capitulation to Stalinism is out of line. It is not. France is accustomed to a variety of revolutionary and counter-revolutionary regimes. Stalinism leads the mass labor movement in France and is unlikely for some time to do more than maintain the democratic regime with some more nationalization.

The Workers Party has added a new theoretical clarification to these tendencies. It has now declared that there hangs a great question mark over the ability of the proletariat to reassemble a revolutionary leadership before it is "destroyed" by disintegrating capitalism.

Under these compulsions slogans such as National Liberation Constituent Assembly, nationalization, for the Labor Party in the United States and all variety of "democratic demands" assume the most conservative not to say reactionary, character. At the back of all this is a conception of the proletariat, learned in the Russian degeneration and fortified by the defeats in Europe.

Trotsky stood for the defense of the degenerated workers state but never except as a theoretical prognosis for the purpose of showing what was evolved, did he adulterate the Bolshevism of the world revolution by the faintest trace of this poison.

C. ECONOMISM

We have elsewhere defined the tendency of Germain as an Economist tendency:

> In 1902 the Economists governed themselves by the economic necessity of large scale production rather than the mobilization of the masses to fight Tsarism and establish their political unification in the democratic dictatorship of the proletariat and peasantry.
> In 1916, the imperialist Economists governed themselves by the economic necessity of supra-national centralization rather than the unification and mobilization of the proletariat and peasantry of the

> oppressed and oppressing countries. In 1918, Bukharin posed the economic necessity of nationalization rather than the mobilization of the Russian masses into their own organizations to control production and safeguard against counter-revolution
>
> What does Germain propose today? In the full Economist tradition adapted to the present situation, he continues to speak of the economically progressive character of nationalization and planned economy. Already in Poland, his position shows the political seriousness of basic error. The Economists of 1902 thought that they were only defending the economic organization of large scale capitalism. In reality they were defending Tsarism because only the revolutionary democratic mobilization of the proletariat and peasantry could destroy political feudalism. The imperialist Economists in 1916 thought they were only defending the economic centralization accomplished by imperialism. In reality they were defending imperialism because only the mobilization of the masses of the oppressed and oppressing countries could destroy national domination. Germain in 1947 thinks he is only defending the nationalization and planned economy of the bureaucracy. In reality, he is defending Stalinism because only the strategic perspective of revolutionary reconstruction by the European masses as a unit, and particularly in Russia, Eastern Europe and Germany, can oppose both the internationalism of Stalinist Russia and the internationalism of American imperialism. No matter how loudly Germain proclaims that Stalinism is the main danger, no matter how he shifts on defeatism or defensism in Russia, he cannot wiggle out of his capitulation to Stalinism so long as he continues to look to economic centralization and planning for social progress. ("The Economist Tendency In the Fourth International.")

The basis for the Economist tendency of Germain lies in its special reaction to Trotsky's heritage. It is the only tendency which tries to maintain "the dual heritage" as a unified world conception under circumstances which demand a development of the theory. The result is that the Germain tendency neither "defends" Russia by Trotsky's method, nor fully advocates the world revolution by Trotsky's method.

It continually vacillates on the defense of the workers' state. It dared not call for the victory of Stalinist Russian over Japanese troops and only the rapid end of the war saved it from the full consequences of its false position. It finally calls for the withdrawal of the troops of the Red Army from the occupied regions, a policy which could not possibly be advocated by a political tendency which had thought through and was willing to face all the implications of its position.

The Red Army and the Kremlin are "introducing" in Germany according to Germain, "progressive property forms through bureaucratic measures." American imperialism, as its maneuvers in regard to the Ruhr show, seeks "to preserve reactionary property forms through reactionary measures." Whenever faced with this choice, says Trotsky, we choose "the lesser evil." The Fourth International cannot choose. The source of these vacillations is rooted deep in theory.

The Russian Proletariat

Shachtman defines the relations of production in Russia as "slavery," a definition of no value whatsoever except that by negation it excludes the Russian proletariat as being prepared for the socialist revolution by the mechanism of production itself. But the tendency of Germain, by insisting that the origin of the Stalinist bureaucracy is in consumption only, implies that the relations of production in Russia are socialist (or transitional to socialism) and thereby makes the revolution of the Russian proletariat a response to "tyranny" and "oppression" or stimulation from external forces. Germain continues to insist that the revolution in Russia is a political revolution. Thus, he and Shachtman exclude a revolution of the Russian proletariat based upon the process of production. The result is that, despite phrases, both in practice exclude the Russian proletariat as a revolutionary force from their calculations of revolution on a world scale.

Shachtman sees the world proletariat essentially through the same defeatist spectacles through which he views the Russian proletariat. He places a big question mark on the whole revolutionary perspective. He hands over the theoretical decision which he has to make to an empirical mysticism which he euphemistically calls "struggle." What is his policy therefore? He holds on to the "democratic" labor bureaucracy as the French Majority holds on to the Stalinist bureaucracy.

They want "a democratic interlude." They want the proletarian revolution to wait until the mass party can guarantee a struggle without possibility of catastrophe.

Germain and his co-thinkers apply to the Russian proletariat the policy that Shachtman applies to the world proletariat. Where Shachtman and Co. hold on to the labor bureaucracy, Germain and his co-thinkers hold on to the nationalized property. They elevate into a policy Trotsky's analogy of the Russian state as a big trade union. Their defensism continues because they are terrified of the proletarian revolution in Russia unless a mass revolutionary party can guarantee that imperialism will not profit by the defeat of the bureaucracy.

Shachtman vacillates between a verbal revolutionism and his actual subordination to the "democratic interlude" of the labor leadership. Germain vacillates between a real revolutionism in Western Europe and the Kremlin and Red Army. Shachtman's revolutionism wrecked against his need to support the bureaucracies of Western Europe Germain's revolutionism is wrecked against his defense of the nationalized property, i.e., the Kremlin and the Red Army.

With the increasing success, i.e. lease on life, of the labor bureaucracy, Shachtman, the petty-bourgeois, becomes more defensist i.e., more Menshevik in his politics. With the increasing success of the Kremlin and the Red Army, however, Germain, a Bolshevik is compelled to become increasingly defeatist in regard to the Kremlin bureaucracy. The great difference lies in the perspective of world proletarian revolution consistently maintained by Germain and questioned by Shachtman. That is why Shachtman, beginning with a conditional defensism in 1941, ends with an unconditional defeatism in regard to Russia based upon a defeatist attitude to the proletariat everywhere. It is the concept of the world proletarian revolution which is driving Germain from a conditional to an unconditional defeatism in regard to the Kremlin and the Red Army.

The vacillations of Shachtman can be cured only by a recognition of the elemental and instinctive drive of the proletariat on a world scale and particularly, in his own country, to reconstruct society on communist beginnings. The vacillations of Germain can be cured only by the recognition of the elemental and instinctive drive of the Russian proletariat to reconstruct society on communist beginnings.

The Vacillations Repeated

But if Russia and "nationalized property" are not adequately defended, the world revolutionary aspect of Trotsky's heritage is not adequately defended either. The vacillation on Russian defense is reflected in the propaganda for the world revolution by the Fourth International.

The concept of the predominant role of the party, learnt in Russia, is transferred to Western Europe. It bases the corruption of the bureaucracies of the Communist Parties on the machinations of the Kremlin and not on the developed antagonisms of the bourgeoisie, the proletariat and the petty-bourgeoisie. Thereby, it is unable to meet on a fundamental class basis the demoralized opportunism of Shachtman and the IKD nor the infantile leftism of Munis.

Its revolutionary propaganda tends to demand certain actions of the proletariat rather than elicit and develop its own proletarian experiences. Hence its embarrassment when these actions do not take place and Shachtman and the I.K.D.'ers demand: where is the revolution you promised?; its unrewarding concentration on issues like the vote on the referendum. As we demonstrated, it promulgates the revolutionary readiness of the masses but cannot motivate it from the objective manifestations as Trotsky did in regard to the union movement in 1919. It announces rather than analyzes. Its revolutionism consists more in exhortation, and in manifestos rather than the concrete daily presentation of the revolutionary program. It does not see the organic unity between the party and the revolutionary masses but is far too much governed by the false idea of Lenin in *What is to be Done* that the party brings socialist consciousness to the masses from the outside – direct result of the theory of the degenerated workers' state. Worse still, Germain now begins to find the consciousness and organization of the proletariat in 1944 lower than it was in 1918. He finds that the phenomenal growth of Stalinism corresponds to the "historic retreat" of the workers movement. If the vacillation on the Russian question is to be corrected by the revision, not the exposition, of Trotsky's theory on Russia, the vacillation on the world revolution is to be corrected by the most resolute struggle for the method of Bolshevism. We shall take as a model the Third Congress of the Comintern, dominated by Trotsky, the same Trotsky who wrote the Transitional Program.

D. THE METHOD OF BOLSHEVISM

In 1921 the Third International recognized that the revolutionary wave which began in October 1917 had passed.

> The first period of the revolutionary movement after the war is characterized by the elemental nature of the onslaught, by the considerable formlessness of its methods and aims and by the extreme panic of the ruling classes; and it may be regarded by and large as terminated.

No such situation exists today. The extreme panic of the ruling-classes is far greater than in 1921. The quotation above continues:

> The class self-confidence of the bourgeoisie and the outward stability of its state organs have undoubtedly become strengthened. The dread of Communism has abated, if not completely disappeared. The leaders of the bourgeoisie are new even boasting about the might of their state apparatus and have everywhere assumed the offensive against the working masses, on both the economic and political fronts.

Now some such period as this is what Trotsky had in mind when he wrote in 1939 that if, during or after the war the proletariat did not succeed in making the revolution and was thrown back on all fronts, then he could not conceive another situation in which it could conquer. If there are those who think that such a situation has now been reached, let them say so and stop their intolerable playing with great questions.

Of the proletariat itself the Theses of the Third Congress state:

> The elements of stability, of conservatism and of tradition, completely upset in social relations, have lost most of their authority over the consciousness of the toiling masses.

We ask: When were the workers all over the world ever so free of all elements of stability, of conservatism, and of tradition? If Stalinism corrupts the revolutionary urge of the masses in 1947, the Social-Democracy corrupted it in 1921. If Stalinism is the extreme corruption that it is, that is because of the extreme revolutionism of the masses. This is strictly in accordance with the laws of social development and is not the product of the Kremlin.

The Theses call the capitalism of 1921 "Capitalism in its death-agony." The whole of world civilization is no longer in its death agony. Putrefaction and gangrene have set in. But the International cannot see this because it persists in seeing progress in the monstrous barbarism of Russia and the spread of this into Europe and Asia.

The Third Congress in its Thesis on Tactics, did not debate the level of consciousness of the masses. It gave freely to the centrists all that they wanted of this. It attributed the failure of the revolution to the treachery of the workers' parties and added further:

> ... it is this which during the period of apparent prosperity of 1919–20 encouraged new hopes in the proletariat of improving its conditions within the framework of capitalism, the essential cause of the defeat of the risings in 1919 and of the decline of the revolutionary movements in 1919–1920.

Take that and do your best with it, Comrade Shachtman and all your co-thinkers. The Congress admitted that: "the majority of the workers is not yet under the influence of communism, above all, in the countries where the power of finance capital is particularly strong and has given birth to vast layers of workers corrupted by imperialism (for example in England and the United States) and where genuine revolutionary propaganda among the masses is just beginning." Most important of all, the greatest fight at this Congress was around rejecting the theory of the offensive and the Congress insisted that there was no possibility of the revolution until the majority of the proletariat accepted the leadership of the Communists

Take it all, Comrade Shachtman and all the rest of you: Invent for 1947 a bourgeoisie confident, vast layers of workers corrupted by imperialism, a majority not accepting revolution, make your reactionary fantasies into a thesis. The International wastes its time and betrays its own vacillations when it argues with you on that basis.

Bolshevism in 1921

It wastes its time. It betrays its own vacillations. Because in 1921 after registering the set-back, the decline of the mass revolts, and the confidence and boasting of the bourgeoisie, the Third Congress then put forward policy. And what was this policy?

> All agitation and propaganda, every action of the Communist Party ought to be **permeated** by this sentiment, that on the capitalist basis, **no durable amelioration** of the condition of the great body of the proletariat is possible; that **only the overthrow of the bourgeoisie and the destruction of the capitalist state** will **make it possible** to work for the improvement of the conditions of the proletariat and to restore the national economy ruined by capitalism.

For 1947, is this Bolshevik policy or not? This is the question that must be answered. But for it to be answered, it must be asked and the example must be set. This is and has been the basic position of the Johnson-Forest Tendency since 1943. Is it sectarianism, ultra-leftism, semi-syndicalism, phrase-mongering? Then let us have it asked and clearly answered on all sides.

The thesis warns that this, of course, should not prevent the struggle for vital, actual and immediate demands of the workers. But these were not to be substituted for the propaganda and agitation for the revolutionary overthrow of bourgeois society. These theses, it should be noted, were not literary or historic surveys. They were written in 1921 to guide the parties until 1922:

> The revolutionary character of the present epoch consists precisely in this that the most modest conditions of existence for the working masses are incompatible with the existence of capitalist society, and that for this reason even the struggle for the most modest demands takes on the proportions of a struggle for communism.

The Task of the Party

The 1921 Theses say that the struggles may be defensive but it is the duty of the party to deepen the defensive struggle, to amplify it and turn it into an offensive.

To the French Party the thesis offered some advice, the reaction against the war was developing more slowly in France than in the other countries. In other words, the French proletariat was more "backward" than the others of continental Europe. The advice of the Third Congress was:

> The practical agitation ought to take a character very much more pointed and more energetic. It ought not to dissipate itself with

> incidental situations and the shifting and variable combinations of daily politics. In all events small or large, the agitation of the party should draw the same fundamental revolutionary conclusions and inculcate them into the working masses even the most backward.

This is Bolshevism. Or is it sectarianism?

In 1922 the Fourth Congress met. It said that fascism, white terror and the state of siege against the proletariat was rising. It said that there was approaching an era of democratic-pacifist illusions, and democratic-pacifist governments in France and Britain. It warned that there were many stages between defeat and victory. It showed that with the decline of the revolutionary wave, the centrists had moved away from the Third International and gone back to the Second. But it did not then begin wailing about the illusions of the masses or speculating on the date of the insurrection. Instead it declared:

> The conception according to which, in the unstable equilibrium of contemporary bourgeois society, the gravest crisis can suddenly burst as the result of a great strike, a colonial uprising or a new war, or even a parliamentary crisis, is even truer today than it was at the time of the Third Congress.
>
> But it is precisely because of this that the 'subjective' factor that is to say, the degree of understanding, of will, of combativity, and of organization of the working class and of its vanguard acquires an enormous importance.
>
> The majority of the working class of the United States and of Europe ought to be won, that is the essential task of the Communist International today as formerly."

The Bolshevism of 1947

Now we ask: If this was Bolshevism in 1921, where is Bolshevism in 1947? A mighty debate shakes the conference halls of the British Congress. On what? Entry or non-entry into the Labor Party. The whole British party, majority and minority, despite superficial differences, is united on the most backward, the most superficial conceptions of the world economy and the crisis in Britain. Under its nose a responsible bourgeois journal writes:

> The severity of the problems that face the country is such that the

> great majority of people would endorse any policy that offered a real prospect of emerging from them. This does not exclude even the extreme forms of Socialism, enforced by dictatorial methods, that are advocated by the 'Keep Left' school.[8]

This is a serious warning **to the International** and can be verified in innumerable ways. The article appeared in the week that the Prime Minister and the Leader of the Opposition warned the British people of a crisis surpassing the crisis of the war. In the same week the Congress debated on the level of: illusions, no illusions; boom, no boom; lull, no lull. For this the International bears the entire responsibility as it does for the shameful and suicidal policies of the French Majority. In a world of great strikes, of continuous parliamentary crises, of colonial revolts on an unheard-of scale, and universal fear of war, in a society where no state has firm foundations under its feet, where all governments leap from one adventure to another, in this world unable to stand still, where all the negative features of 1921 are multiplied ten times over and the positive features have disappeared, here the International, in not one single document or discussion can face the Menshevik tendencies even with the Bolshevism of 1921, far less with what is required in 1947.

The inevitable result could have been foretold. Organizational and petty political problems such as entry or non-entry become dividing lines and the Russian question becomes a football in which extreme right and extreme left maneuver, each for its own purposes, wholesome or otherwise.

Yet even with this disorder rampant in its ranks the International is politically unable to defend Bolshevism for our epoch and differentiate itself from other tendencies. In July–August 1947, it publishes an editorial in the journal *Quatrieme International* with the portentous title "New Stage." The new stage is not as in 1921, the recognition of defeat. No, it is quite the reverse.

> For the first time since the "liberation," the proletariat (in France, Belgium, Italy and Holland) has taken the field in a vast class movement, conquering inertia and even the opposition of the

8 *The Economist*, August 16, 1947.

> bureaucratic apparatus of the Stalinist and reformist leadership, and partially disrupting them.
>
> There has taken place a sharp break, very important, above all from the consequences which it will have in the near future, between large layers of the proletarian vanguard and these leaderships. The experience acquired by the masses which have joined the battle with such vitality and dynamism in the great struggles of the past weeks will serve to reinforce the rapidity of revolutionary emergence from the treacherous tutelage of Stalinism and reformism.

Here in the midst of the greatest dislocation of society ever known is a great movement of the proletariat on a continental scale accompanied by vast colonial movements in the Near East, the Far East and Africa. But the conclusion betrays the un-Leninist vacillation and timidity.

> Finally, after carefully weighing everything, one is **compelled** to conclude that we probably have before us a period of at least some years during which no decision will be arrived at either in the sphere of war or in the sphere of triumphant Revolution, but which will be characterized by the instability of the bourgeoisie, by great economic and political difficulties, by convulsions and crisis, and which will unloose, in the inevitable struggles which will be waged by the world proletariat and the colonial peoples, new revolutionary forces freed from Stalinist tutelage.

The writer is "compelled to conclude" that we probably have before us a period of "**at least some years**."

What is this doing here? All the centrists, Shachtman in the lead, will pounce upon this, declaring that this is what they have been saying when in reality they have been saying something fundamentally different Whoever promised the victorious revolution as the overthrow of capitalism on a world or at least a continental scale except after long years of advancing and retreating struggle?

This passage in this place is a concession, one of the perpetual concessions to the centrists which they use to advance their own reactionary policies. Trotsky said in 1938 to the American comrades: You may be perfectly able to conquer the power in ten years. Therefore begin the revolutionary preparation for the masses now. And when Shachtman in 1938 thought as he still thinks that the time for revolutionary slogans is when the seizure of power was approaching Trotsky shouted at him, "How can we in such a critical situation as now exists in the whole world, in the U. S. measure the stage of development of the workers' movements?"

We ask these editorial writers the same: How can you, in the situation of 1947 measure the development of "the new stage"? Either the statement means nothing except what every Marxist knows since Marx's thesis of 1850, (it can be found in the Thesis of the Third Congress) or it is a political capitulation. Every line of the Third Congress is directed against precisely this "some years before the revolution" thesis, the political haven of left Menshevism.

Immediately after this the editorial swings away to the left.

> The new stage is above all marked by the **broadest** and most **fertile** intervention of the proletariat, which **upsets all** the calculations of the bourgeoisie and **of the Stalinist bureaucracy**...

The words we have underlined should not be written if they are not meant. But before the sentence is over we are on the right again.

> ... which can and must decide the historic alternative, not in the direction of war but in that of the world socialist revolution.

The revolution is opposed not to the counter-revolution but to the war. That is precisely what all defeatists do and the extreme rightists are now doing.

Finally to clinch the confusion, the editorial ends as follows:

> It is for us, world movement of the Fourth International, to unfold before the oppressed masses of the world, clearly, audaciously, this perspective of the possible preparation of the Revolution which can prevent the war and lead tortured mankind from the impasse and the toils in which it is plunged by imperialism and the soviet bureaucracy...

The war again is posed as alternative to the "possible" preparation of the revolution. We prefer not to try to explain what this means. But the last sentence cannot be ignored.

> The new stage into which we enter is that of the hardening of the revolutionary forces for the preparation, slow perhaps, but sure, of the Revolution.

All Can Agree on "Slow But Sure"

That last sentence is a political catastrophe. Shachtman, the French Majority, the British Party, the I.K.D., every conservative tendency in the International can hold to their positions and **agree completely with this**. How does one carry out a preparation, slow, perhaps, but sure for a revolution! The difference lies then in the perhaps. Shachtman is absolutely certain that the preparation will be slow. Some of his closest supporters think it will be twenty years. Otherwise, despite the great question-mark, Shachtman, who is liberal about these things, will be willing to be sure of the ultimate revolution just as long as the preparation is slow. And if, now that the proletariat in one great series of strikes has "upset all the calculations of the bourgeoisie and of the Stalinist bureaucracy," if with this new stage, we declare that now the preparation is to be slow (perhaps) but sure, then during the two previous years when the proletariat did not advance to the new stage what exactly should have been the tempo of the preparation – presumably extremely slow and conversely extremely sure.

During two years the centrifugal elements in the International have with no slowness at all, (here they are never slow) and with a growing sureness, gathered their reactionary forces and are now declaring themselves. At this time, when the International, on the basis of the new stage, should have swept this continual setting the time for the revolution into the dustbin[9] and met them with the stiffest and most uncompromising programmatic counter-attack, this is the time it chooses to dally with them and in addition to statistics of boom, offers them united fronts on the time-table of the revolution. The insurrection will come when it will come, the world revolution will triumph in the whole world or in part in its own time. This has been and can be legitimate subject for discussion. But only after there is programmatic

9 The Johnson-Forest Tendency met this same reactionary pre-occupation with perspectives of boom from the Workers Party Majority in 1946. We categorically refused to substitute the red herring of discussion on boom for the strategic questions.

agreement. These questions, when raised in the midst of a world crisis never mean what they say on the surface but are a cover for retreat and reaction. Our task is to recognize, in the words of the Third Congress:

> The revolutionary character of the present epoch consists precisely in this that the most modest conditions of the masses are incompatible with the existence of capitalist society and that for this reason even the struggle for the most modest demands takes on the proportions of a struggle for communism.

How is it possible in the face of this to tell the workers about the slow but sure preparation of the revolution. They are then slowly but surely to starve and shiver without houses, without clothes, and without fuel.

Over and over again, in reading the debates between right and left we are reminded of the pregnant words of Chaulieu and Montal, French Minorityites: "Only the vocabulary distinguishes Frank from Geoffroy."

The basis, the spearhead of Bolshevism in our time is the uncompromising presentation of the need and the methods of social revolution. Nothing else can be the basis. It is the lack of this basis which make it sometimes almost impossible to distinguish right from left at some plenum debates except by the names of the speakers. And this feebleness is not accidental. We can only repeat. It is the Russian position which holds back the International from making a Bolshevik use of the Transitional Program.

E. THE TRANSITIONAL PROGRAM TODAY

It has been necessary to establish the method of Bolshevism, because of the fate that has overtaken the Transitional Program of Trotsky. The Transitional Program is one of the great documents of Marxism, Bolshevism of our time. Yet it is being made the vehicle for the most reactionary theory and practice.

We shall here show what it was, what it is and to what degree 1947 has made readjustments and extensions necessary.

The Transitional Program of 1938 was a program for the "**systematic mobilization of the masses for the proletarian revolution.**"

Except on this basis the Transitional Program could not have abolished the old distinction between the minimal demands and the maximum demands by linking **"day-to-day work...indissolubly... with the actual tasks of the revolution.**"

All minimal demands must be linked to factory committees, for workers' control of production and workers' militia. These are precisely what separated the Transitional Program from the old minimum program anybody can demand anything. It is the method that makes the demands of the Transitional Program transitory to the proletarian revolution. Demands for workers' control of production and workers' militia are not demands on the bourgeoisie but on the proletariat to prepare it for the proletarian revolution.

The Transitional Program was to implant the idea into the minds of the comrades of "the general (i.e., profoundly revolutionary) character and tempo of our epoch."

> In our minds it, the slogan of workers and farmers government, leads to the "dictatorship of the proletariat."

The transitional demands became revolutionary in fact "insofar" as they "**become demands of the masses as the proletarian government**": i.e., insofar as the masses take over control of production and form themselves into workers' militia, workers' and farmers' government. The Transitional Program is a program for the arming of the workers , a program with the Soviets in mind.

Trotsky was no putschist. He said repeatedly that these were "ideas" to be implanted as propaganda. But not a line in the program is to be seen except as an idea which only awaited mass mobilization to be transplanted into revolutionary action of the most violent kind. The military program is a case in point. The program says simply:

> Military training and arming of workers and farmers under direct control of workers and farmers' committees; creation of military schools for the training of commanders among the toilers, chosen by workers' organization; substitution for the standing army of a people's militia, indissolubly linked up with factories, mines, farms, etc.

In those simple sentences the leader of the October Revolution and the organizer of the Red Army was preparing the revolutionary proletariat to split the bourgeois army, take over a section of it, organize it as a Red Army, build up a proletarian force and then arm the whole population. This is the significance of the Transitional Program.

1938 and 1947

The position of the Johnson-Forest tendency is clear. For us the main difference between 1938 and 1947 can be summed up in two concepts:

I. It is the task of the Fourth International to drive as clear a line between bourgeois nationalization and proletarian nationalization as the revolutionary Third International drove between bourgeois democracy and proletarian democracy.

II. The strategic orientation is the unification of proletarian struggle on an international scale as exemplified in the struggle for the Socialist United States of Europe.

This understood we shall take the key features of the program as it was in 1938 and compare it as a program for 1947.

"THE OBJECTIVE PREREQUISITES FOR A SOCIALIST REVOLUTION"

1938 "The world political situation as a whole is chiefly characterized by a historical crisis of the leadership of the proletariat."

This is the key sentence of the Transitional Program. Why?

> Democratic regimes, as well as fascist, stagger on from one bankruptcy to another.
>
> The bourgeoisie itself sees no way out...
>
> In countries where it has already been forced to stake its last upon the card of fascism, it now toboggans with closed eyes toward an economic and military catastrophe.
>
> In the historically-privileged countries... all of capital's traditional parties are in a state of perplexity, bordering on a paralysis of will.
>
> International relations present no better picture...

This is the classic formula for the pre-revolutionary situation. The bourgeoisie cannot govern in the old way. That is why "The historical crisis of mankind is reduced to the crisis of the revolutionary leadership."

1947 The war has come. There is not one single regime, bourgeois-democratic, social-democratic, or military occupation, to which 1938 would not seem a paradise. There is no longer perplexity, there is only terror and fear. The problems are insoluble.

From the bourgeoisie Trotsky now passes to the proletariat.

"THE PROLETARIAT AND ITS LEADERSHIP"

1938 "The economy, the state, the politics of the bourgeoisie and its international relations are completely blighted by a social crisis, characteristic of a pre-revolutionary state of society."

1947 The economy, the state and the politics of the bourgeoisie and its international relations are no longer completely blighted as in 1938. Barbarism is already eating away at the heart of European civilization and the colonial periphery. The regimes of Stalin and his satellites surpass the traditional bourgeois regimes only in the depth of the decline and the hypocrisy of their rulers.

1938 "In all countries, the proletariat is wracked by a deep disquiet. In millions, the masses again and again move onto the road of the revolutionary outbreaks. But each time they are blocked by their own conservative apparatus."

1947 Since 1938 the proletariat and the peasantry have repeatedly shaken decaying bourgeois society to the ground as in country after country during 1944 or paralyzed it with mighty convulsions as in the great strikes of the United States. But the conservative apparatuses have picked up prostrate bourgeois society, set it on its feet again and are holding it together. Without them bourgeois society would not exist.

1938 "The definite passing over of the Comintern to the side of the bourgeois order, its cynically counter-revolutionary role throughout the world, particularly in Spain, France, the United States and other "democratic" countries, created exceptional supplementary difficulties for the world proletariat... The laws of history are stronger than the bureaucratic apparatus. No matter how the methods of the social-betrayers differ – from the social legislation of Blum to the judicial frame-ups of Stalin – they will never succeed in breaking the revolutionary will of the proletariat."

1947 The reformist bureaucracy precisely because it is reformist can no longer hold the allegiance of the masses. They have poured by the hundreds of thousands and the millions into the Communist Parties, thereby declaring as never before, their understanding of the need for a revolutionary transformation of society. But convinced of the bankruptcy of the national bourgeoisie and the national state and in terrible fear of the proletarian revolution, the Comintern seeks to create in Europe and Asia national satellites of Stalinist Russia with the Red Army as its main protector against proletarian uprisings within and intervention from without. In vain. No sign of stabilization appears. The new regimes are driven along the road of totalitarianism. The parties of the Comintern seek to corrupt the revolutionary will of the masses by the prejudices of the petty bourgeoisie, bringing into play all the treacherous devices learnt in the school of the Kremlin. But already the masses have in all spheres shown their capacity to confound and upset the most carefully laid calculations of the leadership. In major countries, already for masses, the term Trotskyism has become synonymous with the idea of revolutionary proletarian struggle for power as opposed to the Kremlin-dominated policies of the Comintern.

It is at this stage that Trotsky in 1938, having established the unbreakable drive to the revolutionary power of the proletariat, distinguishes between the Transitional Program and the minimum program. Trotsky then talks of the necessary question of tactics. But here 1947 is not 1938.

Today the proletariat faces and knows that it faces an economy and social order so shattered that nothing but the most unparalleled efforts can destroy the counter-revolution, rebuild the economy and finally extinguish the spreading flames of war. Every passing day shows to the proletariat that its nearest every-day immediate needs can be satisfied only by actions of the most far-reaching historical character. The struggle for power therefore becomes the main objective of the revolutionary education of the masses.

WAR AND THE ARMING OF THE PROLETARIAT

1938 "The present crisis can sharpen the class struggle to an extreme point and bring nearer the moment of denouement. But that does not mean that a revolutionary situation comes on at one stroke. Actually, its approach is signalized by a continuous series of convulsions. One of these is the wave of sit-down strikes. The problem of the sections of the Fourth International is to help the

proletarian vanguard understand the general character and tempo of our epoch and to fructify in time the struggle of the masses with ever more resolute and militant organizational measures.

"Strike pickets are the basic nuclei of the proletarian army." This is our point of departure. In connection with every strike and street demonstration, it is imperative to propagate the necessity of creating workers' groups for self-defense. It is necessary to write this slogan into the program of the revolutionary wing of the trade unions. It is imperative wherever possible, beginning with the youth groups, to organize groups for self-defense, to drill and acquaint them with the use of arms.

"A new upsurge of the mass movement should serve not only to increase the number of these units but also to unite them according to neighborhoods, cities, regions. It is necessary to give organized expression to the valid hatred of the workers toward scabs and bands of gangsters and fascists. It is necessary to advance the slogan of a workers' militia as the one serious guarantee for the inviolability of workers' organizations, meetings and press."

This does not depend on the consciousness of the masses. It is precisely the consciousness of the masses which is to be altered.

"Only with the help of such systematic, persistent, indefatigable, courageous agitational and organizational work, always on the basis of the experience of the masses themselves, is it possible to root out from their consciousness the traditions of submissiveness and passivity...."

1947 The objective conditions of 1947, the great experiences of military and class warfare that the proletariat has gone through since 1938 makes the 1938 point of departure inadequate. Today in large areas of the world the point of departure is the arming of the proletariat. The slogan of a workers' militia embodying the whole population, men and women, is needed not for defense but as the basis of the seizure of power, a new form of state administration and the reconstruction of the national economy.

ALLIANCE OF WORKERS AND FARMERS

On the same revolutionary scale is the program for the alliance of the workers and farmers. In 1938 there is not one word of parliamentarism in the hundreds of words devoted to this.

1938 "Committees elected by small farmers should make then appearance on the national scene and jointly with workers' committees and committees of bank employees take into their hands control of transport, credit, and mercantile operations affecting agriculture."

1947 The vanguard, in the face of the starving nation, summons the proletariat to lead the nation and particularly the farmers, to overthrow the bourgeois regime in order to begin the reconstruction of the economy.

WORKERS CONTROL OF PRODUCTION

1938 "The working out of even the most elementary economic plan – from the point of view of the exploited, not the exploiters – is impossible without workers' control, that is, without the penetration of the workers' eye into all open and concealed springs of capitalist economy. Committees representing individual business enterprises should meet at conferences to choose corresponding committees of trusts, whole branches of industry, economic regions and finally, of national industry as a whole. Thus, workers' control becomes a school for planned economy. On the basis of the experience of control, the proletariat will prepare itself for direct management of nationalized industry when the hour for that eventuality strikes."

1947 The workers no longer need to penetrate into any of the Springs of capitalist economy. In some of the most important countries of the world the ruin and thievery of capitalist economy are open secrets to the workers. Workers' control of production by an derail plan becomes the sole means whereby it would be possible to rebuild the ruined nationalized economy.

The ruin of the economy is complemented by the demonstrated need and desires of millions of workers to finish once and for all with the slavery of capitalist production and to exercise to the full the vast productive capacities created in them by capitalism, the experience of the Russian Revolution has proved beyond a shadow of doubt that workers' control of production is the deepest expression of proletarian democracy and that without it, it is impossible to solve the basic antagonisms of value production.

1938 "The necessity of advancing the slogan of expropriation in the course of daily agitation in partial form, and not only in our propaganda in its more comprehensive aspects, is dictated by the fact that different branches of industry are on different levels of development, occupy a different place in the life of society, and pass through different stages of the class struggle. Only a general revolutionary upsurge of the proletariat can place the complete expropriation of the bourgeoisie on the order of the day. The task of transitional demands is to prepare the proletariat to solve this problem."

1947 The crisis of national economies like those of France and Britain compel the immediate expropriation of all the basic industries of the national economy by the armed proletariat. Piecemeal expropriation with or without compensation is doomed to failure. Far from agitating for the partial expropriation of individual industries, the need now is for total expropriation under workers' control and comprehensive plans for the integration of national economies into an international production. Not only the ruin of the economy but the capitulation of the impotent bourgeoisie to the need for internationalization forms a sure basis for the agitation and propaganda of international social construction.

The "Marshall Plan" forms the latest climax to the need for a plan of the invading socialist society, imposing itself on the capitalist productive forces. Precisely because of their capitalist nature all such plans can result ultimately in nothing else but disruption of the world economy, increased drive to war and the degradation of the world proletariat.

To these pseudo-international plans of the bourgeoisie the vanguard in every country and particularly in the United States must aim at preparing the proletariat for a genuinely international action: workers' control of the main sources of production, international workers' control of all means of transport; an international plan for the reconstruction of the world economy upon a socialist basis.

Without such plans the proletariat is weakened before the reactionary and malignant manipulation by the bourgeoisie of the inherent need of the productive forces to be organized on an international socialist basis. Above all, the vanguard exposes the worldwide counter-revolutionary role of American imperialism and the hypocritical character of its economic "gifts."

1938 **"However, the state-ization of the banks will produce these favorable results only if the state power itself passes completely from the hands of the exploiters into the hands of the toilers."**

1947 Only if the nationalization takes place under the workers' control of production and the state power in the hands of the toilers, will the statification of banks and other basic industries produce anything except frustration, demoralization and ultimately penal labor for the working class. The slogans of workers' control of production, nationalization can no longer he used except as Lenin used them, in the closest relation with the slogan of a workers' and farmers' government, on the road to the dictatorship of the proletariat.

THE U.S.S.R. AND PROLETARIAN REVOLUTION

1938 **"From this perspective, impelling concreteness is imparted to the question of the 'defense of the USSR.' If tomorrow the bourgeois-fascist grouping the 'faction of Butenko,' so to speak, should attempt the conquest of power, the 'faction of Reiss' inevitably would align itself on the opposite side of the barracades. Although it would find itself temporarily the ally of Stalin, it would nevertheless defend not the Bonapartist clique but the social base of the USSR, i.e., the property wrenched away from the capitalists and transformed into state property. Should the 'faction of Butenko' prove to be in alliance with Hitler, then the 'faction of Reiss' would defend the USSR from military intervention, inside the country as well as on the world arena. Any other course would be a betrayal."**

1947 The rise of Russia as a vast state-capitalist trust, driven by the contradictions of capitalist production and the struggle for the control of the world market, has rendered obsolete prognoses about elements in the Stalinist bureaucracy who seek the restoration of private property. Neither the tendencies in world economy nor the economic and social development of the U.S.S.R. itself, gives the slightest indication of any tendency towards the restoration of private property. The bureaucracy defends the state property and will continue to defend it. It no longer confines itself to the reactionary utopia of safeguarding socialism in a single country. Allied to the Communist

Parties, it is a serious contender for world power and its very existence is the greatest source of corruption of the world proletariat. It is the greatest counter-revolutionary force in the world today. No remnant of the October Revolution remains. And the Russian proletariat in particular, and the world proletariat in general, must make no distinction whatever between Russian state-capitalism and American imperialism as the enemies of the proletariat and the chief torturers and oppressors and deceivers of hundreds of millions of workers and peasants. Above all, the vanguard pursues with the utmost relentlessness any theory which implies that a state reorganization of property by any agency whatever contains in it anything else but an intensification of the fundamental antagonisms of capitalist production and the degradation of all classes in society. If bases itself unshakably upon the theoretical conception, now demonstrated in practice, that the only solution to the antagonism of capitalist production is the creative power of the modern worker relieved from the status of proletarian.

1938 "A revision of planned economy from top to bottom in the interests of producers and consumers. Factory committees should be returned the right to control production. A democratically organized consumers' cooperative should control the quality and price of products."

1947 The planned economy of Stalinist Russia cannot be revised. The proletariat alone through its factory committees, its free trade unions and its own proletarian party can plan the economy. All other plans consist first and foremost of terror against the proletariat, the chief of the productive forces, to enforce submission to the unresolved fundamental antagonisms of capitalist production. The antagonisms are insoluble except by instituting proletarian democracy.

THE FOURTH INTERNATIONAL AND THE PROLETARIAT

1938 "Of course, even among the workers who had at one time risen to the first ranks, there are not a few tired and disillusioned ones. They will remain, at least for the next period, as by-standers. When a program or an organization wears out, the generation which carried it on its shoulders wears out with it. The movement is revitalized by the youth who are free of responsibility for the past.

The Fourth International pays particular attention to the young generation of the proletariat. All of its policies strive to inspire the youth with belief in its own strength and in the future. Only the fresh enthusiasm and aggressive spirit of the youth can guarantee the preliminary successes in the struggle; only these successes can return the best elements of the older generation to the road of revolution. Thus it was, thus it will be."

1947 The Fourth International does not confound its own forces with the objective revolutionary situation and the movement of the proletariat. Precisely because of its small forces, it addresses itself always to the vanguard of the proletariat, particularly the youth. By placing before them the revolutionary program in all its amplitude but based always on concrete circumstances and experiences, it wins over the most aggressive elements who in turn will lead the less advanced layers in revolutionary struggle. The fourth International rejects without reservation all plans to base revolutionary policy upon the backwardness of the masses or the smallness of the Bolshevik Party.

1938 "Without inner democracy – no revolutionary education. Without discipline – no revolutionary action. The inner structure of the Fourth International is based on the principles of democratic centralism; full freedom in discussion, complete unity in action."

1947 The crisis of humanity sharpens all contradictions, even those within the revolutionary movement itself. Never was it more necessary for the international party of world socialism to practice the most ruthless freedom of discussion. Never was it more necessary to have the most rigid discipline in action. Theoretical intransigeance must be combined with organizational flexibility. At the moment when the proletariat is in process of making a great historic advance, sects, historically progressive in periods of quiescence, become reactionary. For all who oppose the democratic imperialisms and Stalinism, unity in one party is essential. The Fourth International will pursue without mercy those enemies of proletarian power who fly the banner of Trotskyism, and yet seek to disrupt the continuity of our movement.

The above is not a program for adoption. Not even a draft program can reasonably come except from an international center the work of comrades of varied knowledge and recent and concrete experiences with the proletariat. But enough has been said to make it impossible:

1) for Menshevism to conceal itself behind a treacherous interpretation of the Transitional Program.

2) for Bolshevism to allow Menshevik tendencies to obscure the fundamentals of our method with picayune disputes aimed at whittling away its revolutionary dynamism, confidence and audacity, demanded now as never before by the objective relations of society. There can be neither right nor left nor centre here. This is Bolshevism and opposed to it are its enemies.

CONCLUSION

We have to draw the theoretical arrow to the head. History has shown that in moments of great social crisis, its farthest flights fall short of the reality of the proletarian revolution. Never was the proletariat so ready for the revolutionary struggle, never was the need for it so great, never was it more certain that the proletarian upheaval, however long delayed, will only the more certainly take humanity forward in the greatest leap forward it has hitherto made. The periods of retreat, of quiescence, of inevitable defeats are mere episodes in the face of the absolute nature of the crisis. Wrote Marx in 1851,

> Proletarian revolutions...criticize themselves constantly, interrupt themselves continually in their own course, come back to the apparently accomplished in order to begin it afresh, deride with unmerciful thoroughness the inadequacies, weaknesses and paltrinesses of their first attempts, seem to throw down their adversary only in order that he may draw new strength from the earth and rise again more gigantic before them, recoil ever and anon from the indefinite prodigiousness of their own aims, until the situation has been created which makes all turning back impossible, and the conditions themselves cry out....

Today from end to end of the world there can be no turning back. But the democratic instincts and needs of hundreds of millions of people are crying out for an expression which only the socialist revolution can give. There is no power on earth that can suppress them. They will not be suppressed.

September 15, 1947

APPENDIX
The Political Economy of Germain

Governing all economic conceptions are certain philosophic conceptions, whether the economists are aware of them or not. And equally governing all political conceptions are certain economic conceptions. Germain's whole analysis of Russia is governed by an economic analysis. It is underconsumptionism.

In his "Draft Theses" (*International Bulletin*, Published by the Socialist Workers Party, p. 13) Germain writes:

> The tendency toward structural assimilation is undeniable. This tendency does not stem from the need for 'internal accumulation of capital,' that is, from any pursuit of profits. It is precisely here that the essential economic difference between capitalist economy and Soviet economy lies. The central problem of capitalist economy is the problem of getting surplus-value – that is to say, the pursuit of profits (under the capitalist system accumulation of capital is the capitalization of the surplus-value; this can be achieved only if surplus-value is gotten). But with Soviet economy the basic question is expansion of production, independently of the matter of profits (the economist Leontiev, in an article published in 1943, acknowledges that between 1928

> and 1935 the Soviet metallurgical industry operated at a steady loss and could not have survived and grown except with the help of state subsidies). Whereas imperialism consists essentially in the search for new spheres of capital investment in order to combat the tendency toward a steady decline in the average rate of profit, Soviet expansionism looks for sources of raw materials, finished goods, etc., independently of the question of profits, considering only the needs of production and of the planned economy.

Germain possesses the virtue of making all his mistakes powerfully and clearly. It is difficult to see how it is possible to make more fantastic mistakes than he concentrates in this passage.

The Soviet metallurgical industry operated at a loss. All that this means is that surplus-labor extracted from one sphere of the economy was used to bolster up another sphere. A capitalist economy, particularly economies that are controlled by the state, does exactly the same thing. There is no special "Soviet virtue" in this. The British state today will have no hesitation whatever in producing in one sphere at a loss in order to bolster such over-all purposes as it has. Germain obviously believes that today a capitalist economy would see a vital industry not grow and even not survive because it could not show a profit on the books.

Germain informs us that "with Soviet economy the basic question is expansion of production, independently of the matter of profits." According to this political economy, Soviet economy just has to produce and produce and produce.

An economy can only produce with what it has. The national production must attend to the absolute needs of the population in the broadest sense; it must renew the worn-out plant and then it can expand only with what remains. Now if as in Russia, it is a poverty-stricken economy functioning within the world-market, the surplus is strictly limited. It must pay the worker at his value, it cannot afford to pay him more. To do so would lessen the precious surplus. And forthwith, it is in the grip of value production.

This is what Marx taught, that once the proletariat is humiliated, degraded, a proletarian, then automatically the only way of raising the productivity of labor is by expanding the constant capital, the machinery, the plant, at the expense of the workers. Stalin would doubtless be delighted to be able to raise "the standard of living" of the Russian workers. He cannot do it. Even where a plant is doing adequate service, the discovery and popularization of a superior type of machinery in Western Europe compels the rapid depreciation in value, i.e., the scrapping of this particular type of production and the substitution of the higher. Stalin does not need to know political economy in order to do this. Self-preservation dictates this constant reorganization of the economy, as far as possible, in order to maintain a reasonable relation with the other economies of the world. When the world-market existed as a functioning communication, this test according to value acted automatically often by violent crises. Today, when the world market is in ruins, the same necessity exists. The planners, particularly in backward Russia, have no guide at all except the most ruthless production of surplus-labor to feed the insatiable needs of the economy. Engels in *Anti-Dühring* summed up Stalin's dilemma with astonishing precision. The state-ownership of capital, he says, possesses the "technical means" of solving the problems of capitalist production. Technically, production in Russia has an unlimited market. It is into this unlimited pit that the under-consumptionists fall and drown themselves. It would, for example, be insanity to produce vast quantities of food and cotton-goods. The wages of workers must be limited. So are the appetites of even Stalinist bureaucrats.

Stalinism cannot produce and produce and produce. It is constantly caught between the contradiction that it cannot get surplus-labor except from labor-power. And it must keep the cost of labor-power as cheap as possible; otherwise the cost of the commodity, i.e. the labor that goes into it rises to a degree that imperils the whole economy in its relation to other economies. Marx took special care to warn of precisely this when he wrote:

> Centralization in a certain line of industry would have reached its extreme limit, if all the individual capitals invested in it would have become amalgamated into one single capital.
>
> This limit would not be reached in any particular society until the entire social capital would be united, either in the hands

> of one single capitalist, or in those of one single corporation."
> (*Capital*, Vol. I, p. 688)

In a given economy, i.e., in a state-capitalist corporation which functioned within the world market, there would be a struggle to maintain a certain relation between constant and variable capital, between industrial plant and labor. And as long as other economies developed their systems, the state-capitalist corporation would have to maintain a similar relation. That is precisely the dilemma of Stalinism. The planning only allows the planners, insofar as they can guess at what is required, to manipulate the economy and the workers the more easily for the production of surplus-value. If, however, the economy were a state-capitalist corporation embracing the whole world, then and only then would the whole problem be altered. The world market would have been abolished. Value production would cease, and if men would stand for it, a plan could work. That, however, would not be capitalism, and as Lenin said, we are a long way from that.

The question could best be illuminated by a few theoretical observations on the "Marshall Plan." If, abstractly speaking, the United States did use its surplus to equip the continent of Europe, in a few-years it would be faced with a modernized economy, so superior to its own that its own products would be driven out of the American market. Forthwith it would find that it needed to struggle now for surplus-value to re-equip its own plant now depreciated, not by wind and rain, but in value. And so it would go.

The mode of appropriation, i.e., by individual private capitalists, undoubtedly created a certain anarchy of production, particularly of the old commercial type of crises. But the basic contradiction is in production, not in the market, and lies in the contradiction between the constant expansion of capital and the relative diminution of labor. It is not the realization of surplus-value but the falling rate of profit, i.e., the falling relation of the total surplus-value to the total social capital. This relation is determined by capital on a world scale and Stalinism can never escape it. In the early days it made a leap but that relation soon caught up with it and now it is trapped.

What is the solution? It is not an extended market. If the world-market for the sale of consumption goods were increased by the discovery of millions of starving people with gold to pay, it would solve nothing. The solution is the raising of the productivity of labor. If capital could double the productivity of labor and make the vast profits of its early days, there are still vast areas of the world to exploit. It does not need Russia. There is China, India, Latin America, Africa. But the margin of profit is so low that expansion on the gigantic scale now required is prohibited to it. Hence it stagnates and foolish capitalists and still more foolish economists then begin to speculate on "raising the standard of living of the workers to provide a market." If capital had depended upon raising the standard of living of the workers as a market, there would have been only one capitalist and he would not have lasted very long.

Marx saw that productivity on the basis of expanding plant and degraded workers would reach a limit. And then he made a tremendous step forward, so tremendous that even now we cannot grasp it. It was made only because his specific economic theories were guided by the dialectical materialist theory. He showed that only by labor itself becoming free could the new levels of productivity be achieved. For him this could not possibly have been a humanitarian flower in the buttonhole of nationalized property. Man, educated, trained by the achievements of capitalism, would raise the productivity of labor by reversing the capitalist method, expansion of plant and degradation of the worker. Only by the increasing development of the worker as a human being, could the capitalist movement be reversed. Bureaucratic collectivism, managerial society, and degenerated workers state, all can plan to the last vitamin. They can never reverse this movement.

The whole question of the Marxist analysis of capitalist crisis has been debated for many years. Lenin, in particular, in debates with the Narodniks at the turn of the century, and later, never tolerated any theories which made the decline of capitalism turn on the realization of surplus value, i.e., market economics. Now the experience of Russia, and in its way, the development of the American proletariat, sets the seal on the debate.

Today this is not a question of theory. The validity of Marx's thesis is proved by the fact that every economy; Stalinist, American and British is faced with the problem of the productivity of labor. The workers are revolting precisely against being made merely the instruments of increasing productivity. Marx saw and stated that the increasing degradation had its affirmative side, the instinct of the workers themselves to take over production and thus carry out the practical solution of what he saw theoretically. This is the inevitable result of value production.

The increase of constant capital not only degrades the workers but must also throw out millions which it must hold in reserve for the increasing bursts of production whether in the old days in ordinary market competition or as today in the competition of war. Stalinist production not only degrades the working class with the same results as in traditional capitalism. Being value production it must also continually throw out millions of workers from production and have them for future spasmodic bursts despite the present decline of the world market. This is the significance of the minions of slave laborers who are no more than the capitalist industrial reserve army of labor.

Unless this is understood as the basis of the capitalist economy, the road is open not only to the misunderstanding of the Stalinist economy but also to basing the revolutionary instincts of the proletariat upon the absence of employment or the need for a "higher standard of living." From this flows the constant preoccupation with boom and stabilization. The perspective of revolution is based upon the most vulgar economist analysis of world economy and of the proletariat. It is the result of an inability to see that today "be his payment high or low," the proletariat has been developed by capitalism to a stage of elemental revolutionism. This impedes all perspective of any serious economic recovery altogether apart from economic statistics. The fulfillment of this revolutionism is precisely what Marx called the real history of humanity. And it is because the real history of humanity is rejecting the capitalist system that the antagonisms are shaking the society to pieces.

Thus Marxian economics itself develops and becomes fused with the irresistible socialization of labor and its political expression in the rising mass movement. Of all this there is not a hint in the political economy of Germain.

This is a brief popular statement. The question has been more adequately dealt with in:

1. *The Development of Capitalism in Russia* by Lenin, Chapter I,

Translated by F. Forest, New International, Oct., Nov., Dec., 1943.
2. *Production for Production's Sake,* by J. R. Johnson, Internal Bulletin of the Workers Party, May, 1940.
3. *A. Restatement of some Fundamentals of Marxism,* by F. Forest, Internal Bulletin of Workers Party, March 1944.
4. "Luxemburg's Theory of Accumulation", by F. Forest, *New International,* April and May, 1946.
J. R. J.

Every Cook Can Govern

Introduction

Celebrations of the 2,500th anniversary of the creation of a democratic society in ancient Greece took place in 1991. Dignitaries from the various Western democracies attended ceremonies in Greece. The hypocrisy of these celebrations seems obvious in light of the fact that modern parliamentary and congressional democracy is, in many ways, a violation of the principles of direct democracy that were established in ancient Athens and that are examined here in C.L.R. James' thought provoking essay.

What passes for democracy in the modern world is generally held in contempt by the citizens of those very countries which call themselves democracies. In this century, the leading democracies, first and foremost the United States, have been involved in two devastating world wars, the pillage of the peoples of Latin America, Africa and Asia, the support of brutal dictatorships whenever it suited their imperial interests, and so on. At the same time, they have been unable to provide all their citizens with the minimum levels of comfort and culture that a modern technological society is clearly able to produce.

The human race, and the world in which we live, is in a desperate situation. Poverty and unemployment, racism, sexism, and bigotry are endemic in the modern world. Two centuries of industrialization have wreaked havoc on the environment. People starve, not because there is no food, but because food is distributed only when it can make a profit. Even the wealthiest nations are ridden with debt. Corruption is common in politics and business. Disease, random violence and homelessness are eating the heart out of every major city on Earth. Work, for most people, continues to be drudgery, with fewer and fewer opportunities for creative initiative.

What does the democracy of ancient Greece tell us about the possibility of transforming this history of death and destruction into a human and humane future for all the people of the world?

The organization known as CORRESPONDENCE first published this pamphlet in 1956 to explore this question. Written by C.L.R. James, the West Indian Marxist who founded the organization, it was originally intended to refute the idea that, somehow, a vanguard party of the left might lead us to a better future. The title of the pamphlet is a reference to Lenin's belief that "every cook must learn to govern" and that government should be administered by every person in the state. This goal could not be achieved in Lenin's Russia. When this pamphlet was first published the fundamental conflict in the world appeared to be that between Soviet Communism and American Capitalism. It was the position of CORRESPONDENCE, however, that the Soviet economy was in fact just another form of capitalism – state capitalism. By one of history's strange coincidences, evidence of the conflict that really divides the world appeared in the very year *Every Cook Can Govern* was published.

In October 1956, in the totalitarian Communist dictatorship of Hungary, the people rose up and demonstrated the possibility of a revolutionary direct democracy in the modern world. A large and growing demonstration of students and intellectuals was under way in a major square in Budapest when it was joined by thousands of Hungarian workers. They proceeded to create workers' councils and, within 48 hours, took over control and direction of all the means of production, service and communication in Hungary. The old Communist government was overthrown. The Hungarian people were working their way toward a new kind of society which was neither Communist (as that was understood in Eastern Europe and the Soviet Union) nor capitalist. There was nothing in Hungarian society that could withstand their attempt to create a new society.

The revolution was overthrown by the invasion of Soviet tanks. The West, led by the United States, took whatever propaganda advantage that it could from the Soviet oppression, but also took care that the Hungarian Revolution would not spread to other countries. Before 1956, Radio Free Europe and Voice of America had called for East Europeans to revolt. After 1956, that call was never heard again. (While the Soviet Union was crushing the Hungarian Revolution, England, France and Israel invaded Egypt in an attempt to steal the Suez Canal.)

The Hungarian Revolution was direct democracy in action in the modern, industrial world. Workers and others did not act through elected representatives, professional politicians. In the workers councils they acted directly and in concert to assume control of their own lives and their own society. All employees of an establishment met at their workplace as often as everyday to make decisions. Delegates were chosen to carry out decisions or to represent the council at citywide or regional bodies. All delegates were subject to immediate recall.

In 1968, something very similar happened in France. The entire working class of the country occupied all the factories in France and came within a hair's breadth of overthrowing the DeGaulle government. In the same year, the people of Czechoslovakia attempted to do the same and were crushed by another Soviet invasion. In 1980, after many years of struggle, direct democracy appeared in Poland in the form of Solidarity. (By the Solidarity of 1980 we do not mean Lech Walesa in 1990 trying to sell Polish factories to American capitalists.)

The world has recently seen the destruction of totalitarian dictatorships in Eastern Europe and the Soviet Union. We need to understand that *the* first blows to weaken the Soviet Empire were struck by the workers of Eastern Europe and, to some extent, Western Europe. Decades of working class resistance, punctuated by revolutionary attempts to assert direct democracy, made Eastern Europe, and then the Soviet Union, ungovernable. The revolutions in these countries – the attempts to create new societies – have only just begun. China's Tiananmen square, the overthrow of military dictatorships in Africa and the crowds at the Russian legislature during the Moscow coup are well-known examples. Less well-known was the 1989 strike of Soviet coal miners. The strike committees became centers of activity for whole communities. Under the slogan "perestroika from below" these committees began to assume political functions.

Western politicians and journalists would have us believe that these battles and sacrifices were somehow intended to replace totalitarian dictatorship and state capitalism with "free enterprise" and what passes for democracy in our countries. They have tried to use the Eastern European drive for freedom to convince us that we live in the best of all possible worlds, and that the greed, corruption, poverty and violence of our society are minor aberrations.

In the West, the differences between politicians are minor and cosmetic. Policies, platforms and promises are marketing tools to entice the electorate. The campaign speech has been reduced to the eight second sound bite. To be successful, politicians must lower their horizons to the next election. The goal of political parties is not to exercise power wisely but only to achieve power and maintain it.

These are not new developments. This is how Engels described the situation in the United States at the end of the last century:

> Nowhere do 'politicians' form a more separate and powerful section of the nation than precisely in North America. There, each of the two major parties which alternately succeed each other in power is itself in turn controlled by people who make a business of politics, who speculate on seals in the legislative assemblies of the Union as well as of the separate slates, or who make a living by carrying on agitation for theft party and on its victory are rewarded with positions. It is well known the Americans have been trying for thirty years to shake off this yoke, which has become intolerable, and bow in spite of it all they continue to sink ever deeper in this swamp of corruption. It is precisely in America that wc see best how thcre takes place this process of the state power making itself independent in relation to society, whose mere instrument it was originally intended to be. Here there exists no dynasty, no nobility, no standing army, beyond the few men keeping watch on the Indians, no bureaucracy with permanent posts or the right to pensions. And nevertheless we find here two great gangs of political

> speculators, who alternately take possession of the state power and exploit it by the most corrupt means and for the most corrupt ends – and the nation is powerless against these two great cartels of politicians, who are ostensibly its servants, but in reality dominate and plunder it.[1]

These flaws in representative democracies are still well known to their peoples. The popular attitude towards politicians is anger and contempt.

In Canada clumsy and secretive attempts by the federal and provincial governments to amend the constitution have led to demands for a constituent assembly composed of non politicians as well as referenda to ratify any changes. In the United States, where half the eligible population refuse to even take part in the charade of the electoral system, disgust with incumbents has sparked proposals to limit the number of terms that federal and state legislators can serve.

While not the direct democracy of the Hungarian Revolution or ancient Greece, these developments show a growing desire to get away from government by professional politicians, which is what representative democracy is.

We do not want to suggest that the democracy of ancient Greece was perfect or that it can easily be copied in the modern world. Greece was burdened by the dual crimes of slavery and the inferior status of women, as were all ancient societies in the Mediterranean basin and in Asia. What distinguished ancient Athens was that, in that society, human beings began to break out and to produce new forms of self-government. That they could not solve all of the evils of that time should not be surprising.

How useful is this example for the huge, industrial societies of today? One of the things which Greece had, to a significant extent, was a sense of community. In our world, that is substantially absent. How do we envision the possibility of a new, free, cooperative society while we are enmeshed in one that is driven by greed and bigotry? The answer does not lie in electing a new set of legislators, or a different political party to replace the discredited old ones. The answer lies in

1 Frederick Engels, *Introduction to The Civil War in France by Karl Marx on the 20th anniversary of the Paris Commune*, March 18, 1891.

seeing in the Hungarian revolution of 1956, the French Revolt of 1968, the Polish Solidarity of 1980, the modern forms of the direct democracy of ancient Athens.

The answer lies in ending the separation of economics and politics. It involves people taking control of their workplaces, their neighborhoods, their communities directly and without mediators. Without bureaucrats, capitalists and managers standing in the way, it should be possible to build a sense of community, of unity, of cooperation. This will obviously provoke tremendous opposition. Hungarian, French and Polish workers confronted the economic, political and military might of their societies. Either we will find the strength and will to do the same or we will sink further into the decay that is now destroying us.

June, 1992

Every Cook Can Govern

A Study of Democracy in Ancient Greece Its Meaning for Today

BY C.L.R. JAMES

DIRECT DEMOCRACY

The Greek form of government was the city-state. Every Greek city was an independent state. At its best, in the city-state of Athens, the public assembly of all the citizens made all important decisions on such questions as peace or war. They listened to the envoys of foreign powers and decided what their attitude should be to what these foreign powers had sent to say. They dealt with all serious questions of taxation, they appointed the generals who should lead them in time of war. They organized the administration of the state, appointed officials and kept check on them. The public assembly of all the citizens was the government.

Perhaps the most striking thing about Greek Democracy was that the administration (and there were immense administrative problems) was organized upon the basis of what is known as sortition, or, more easily, selection by lot. The vast majority of Greek officials were chosen by a method which amounted to putting names into a hat and appointing the ones whose names came out.

Now the average CIO bureaucrat or Labor Member of Parliament in Britain would fall in a fit if it was suggested to him that any worker selected at random could do the work that he is doing, but that was precisely the guiding principle of Greek Democracy. And this form of government is the government under which flourished the greatest civilization the world has ever known.

Modern parliamentary democracy elects representatives and these representatives constitute the government. Before the democracy came into power, the Greeks had been governed by various forms of government, including government by representatives. The democracy knew representative government and rejected it. It refused to believe that the ordinary citizen was not able to perform practically all the business of government. Not only did the public assembly of all the citizens keep all the important decisions in its own hands. For the Greek, the word isonomia, which meant equality, was used interchangeably for democracy. For the Greek, the two meant the same thing. For the Greek, a man who did not take part in politics was an *idiotes*, an idiot, from which we get our modern word idiot, whose meaning, however, we have limited. Not only did the Greeks choose all officials by lot, they limited their time of service. When a man had served once, as a general rule, he was excluded from serving again because the Greeks believed in rotation, everybody taking his turn to administer the state.

INTELLECTUALS

Intellectuals like Plato and Aristotle detested the system. And Socrates thought that government should be by experts and not by the common people. For centuries, philosophers and political writers, bewildered by these Greeks who when they said equality meant it, have either abused this democracy or tried to explain that this direct democracy was suitable only for the city-state. Large modern communities, they say, are unsuitable for such a form of government.

We of CORRESPONDENCE believe that the larger the modern community, the more imperative it is for it to govern itself by the principle of direct democracy (it need not be a mere copy of the Greek). Otherwise we face a vast and ever-growing bureaucracy. That is why a study, however brief, of the constitution and governmental procedures of Greek Democracy is so important for us today.

Let us see how Greek Democracy administered justice.

The Greek cities for a time had special magistrates and judges of a special type, like those that we have today. When the democracy came into power, about the middle of the 5th Century B.C., there began and rapidly developed a total reorganization of the system of justice. The quorum for important sessions of the assembly was supposed to be 6,000. The Greek Democracy therefore at the beginning of each year, chose by lot 12 groups of 500 each. These 500 tried the cases and their decisions were final.

The Greek Democracy made the magistrate or the judge into a mere clerk of the court. He took the preliminary information and he presided as an official during the case. But his position as presiding officer was merely formal. The jury did not, as in our courts today, decide only on the facts and look to him for information on the law. They decided on the law as well as on the facts. Litigants pleaded their own case, though a litigant could go to a man learned in the law, get him to write a speech and read it himself. The Greeks were great believers in law, both written and unwritten. But the democrats believed not only in the theory of law, but in the principles of equity and we can define equity as what would seem right in a given case in the minds of 500 citizens chosen by lot from among the Athenian population.

NO EXPERTS

He would be a very bold man who would say that that system of justice was in any way inferior to the modern monstrosities by which lawyers mulct the public, cases last interminably, going from court to court, and matters of grave importance are decided by the position of full stops and commas (or the absence of them) in long and complicated laws and regulations which sometimes have to be traced through hundreds of years and hundreds of law books. When the Russian Revolution took place and was in its heroic period, the Bolsheviks experimented with People's Courts. But they were timid and in any case, none of these experiments lasted for very long. The essence of the Greek method, here as elsewhere, was the refusal to hand over these things to experts, but to trust to the intelligence and sense of justice of the population at large, which meant of course a majority of the common people.

THE ORGANIZATION OF GOVERNMENT

We must get rid of the idea that there was anything primitive in the organization of the government of Athens. On the contrary, it was a miracle of democratic procedure which would be beyond the capacity of any modern body of politicians and lawyers, simply because these believe that when every man has a vote, equality is thereby established. The assembly appointed a council of 500 to be responsible for the administration of the city and the carrying out of decisions.

But the council was governed by the same principle of equality. The city was divided into 10 divisions and the year was divided into 10 periods. Each section of the city selected by lot 50 men to serve on the council. All the councillors of each section held office for one tenth of the year. So that 50 people were always in charge of the administration. The order in which the group of 50 councillors from each section of the city should serve was determined by lot. Every day, the 50 who were serving chose someone to preside over them and he also was chosen by lot. If on the day that he was presiding, the full assembly of all the citizens met, he presided at the assembly.

The council had a secretary and he was elected. But he was elected only for the duration of one tenth of the year. And (no doubt to prevent bureaucracy) he was elected not from among the 50, but from among the 450 members of the council who were not serving at the time.

When members had served on the council, they were forbidden to serve a second time. Thus every person had a chance to serve. And here we come to one of the great benefits of the system. After a number of years, practically every citizen had had an opportunity to be a member of the administration. So that the body of citizens who formed the public assembly consisted of men who were familiar with the business of government.

No business could be brought before the assembly except it had been previously prepared and organized by the council.

When decisions had been taken, the carrying out of them was entrusted to the council.

The council supervised all the magistrates and any work that had been given to a private citizen to do.

The Greeks had very few permanent functionaries. They preferred to appoint special boards of private citizens. Each of these boards had its own very carefully defined sphere of work. The coordination of all these various spheres of work was carried out by the council. A great number of special commissions helped to carry out the executive work. For example, there were 10 members of a commission to see after naval affairs, and 10 members of a commission to hear complaints against magistrates at the end of their term. One very interesting commission was the commission for the conduct of religious ceremonies. The Greeks were a very religious people. But most of the priests and officials of the temples were elected and were for the most part private citizens. The Greeks would not have any bunch of Bishops, Archbishops, Popes and other religious bureaucrats who lived by organizing religion. Some of these commissions were elected from the council. But others again were appointed by lot.

At every turn we see the extraordinary confidence that these people had in the ability of the ordinary person, the grocer, the candlestick maker, the carpenter, the sailor, and the tailor. Whatever the trade of the individual, whatever his education, he was chosen by lot to do the work the state required.

And yet they stood no nonsense. If a private individual made propositions in the assembly which the assembly considered frivolous or stupid, the punishment was severe.

DEMOCRATIC DRAMA

Here is some idea of the extent to which the Greeks believed in democracy and equality. One of the greatest festivals in Greece, or rather in Athens, was the festival of Dionysus, the climax of which was the performance of plays for four days, from sunrise to evening. The whole population came out to listen. Officials chose the different playwrights who were to compete. On the day of the performance, the plays were performed and, as far as we can gather, the prizes were at first given by popular applause and the popular vote. You must remember that the dramatic companies used to rehearse for one year and the successful tragedians were looked upon as some of the greatest men in the state, receiving immense honor and homage from their fellow citizens. Yet it was the public, the general public, of 15 or 20 thousand people that came and decided who was the winner.

Later, a committee was appointed to decide. Today such a committee would consist of professors, successful writers and critics. Not among the Greeks. The committee consisted first of a certain number of men chosen by lot from each section of the city. These men got together and chose by lot from among themselves 10 men. These 10 men attended as the judges. At the end of the performances, they made their decision. The 10 decisions were placed in the hat. Five were drawn out. And the one who had the highest vote from among these five received the prize. But even that does not give a true picture of the attitude of the Greeks towards democracy.

Despite the appointment of this commission, there is evidence that the spectators had a preponderant influence on the judges. The Greek populace behaved at these dramatic competitions as a modern crowd behaves at some football or baseball game. They were violent partisans. They stamped and shouted and showed their likes and dislikes in those and similar ways. We are told that the judges took good care to notice the way in which popular opinion went. Because, and this is typical of the whole working of the democracy on the day after the decision, the law allowed dissatisfied citizens to impeach the members of the commission for unsatisfactory decisions. So that the members of the commission (we can say at least) were very much aware of the consequences of disregarding the popular feeling about the plays.

Yet it was the Greeks who invented playwriting. In Aeschylus, Sophocles and Euripides, they produced three tragedians who, to this day, have no equals as practitioners of the art which they invented. Aristophanes has never been surpassed as a writer of comic plays. These men obviously knew that to win the prize, they had to please the populace. Plato, the great philosopher, was, as can easily be imagined, extremely hostile to this method of decision. But the Greek populace gave the prize to Aeschylus 13 times. They were the ones who repeatedly crowned Aeschylus and Sophocles, and later Euripides, as prize winners. It is impossible to see how a jury consisting of Plato and his philosopher friends could have done any better. There you have a perfect example of the Greek attitude to the capacities, judgment and ability to represent the whole body of citizens, which they thought existed in every single citizen.

SLAVERY AND WOMEN

There are many people today and some of them radicals and revolutionaries who sneer at the fact that this democracy was based on slavery. So it was, though we have found that those who are prone to attack

Greek Democracy on behalf of slavery are not so much interested in defending the slaves as they are in attacking the democracy. Frederick Engels in his book on the family makes an analysis of slavery in relation to Greek Democracy and modern scholars on the whole agree with him. In the early days, Greek slavery did not occupy a very prominent place in the social life and economy of Greece. The slave was for the most part a household slave. Later, the slaves grew in number until they were at least as many as the number of citizens.

In later years, slavery developed to such a degree, with the development of commerce, industry, etc., that it degraded free labor. And it is to this extraordinary growth of slavery and the consequent degradation of free labor that Engels attributes the decline of the great Greek Democracy.[2]

However, it is necessary to say this. In the best days of the democracy, there were many slaves who, although denied the rights of citizenship, lived the life of the ordinary Greek citizen. There is much evidence of that. One of the most important pieces of evidence is the complaint of Plato that it was impossible to tell a slave to go off the pavement to make way for a free citizen (especially so distinguished a citizen as Plato) for the simple reason that they dressed so much like the ordinary citizen that it was impossible to tell who was a citizen and who was a slave. In fact, Plato so hated Greek Democracy that he complained that even the horses and the asses in the streets walked about as if they also had been granted liberty and freedom. Near the end of the period of radical democracy, Demosthenes, the greatest of Athenian orators, said that the Athenians insisted on a certain code of behavior towards the slaves, not because of the slaves, but because a man who behaved in an unseemly manner to another human being was not fit to be a citizen. There were horrible conditions among the slaves who worked in the mines. But on the whole, the slave code in Athens has been described by competent authorities as the most enlightened the world has known.

---

2 This conventional view on the role of slavery in classical Greece has been challenged in recent years. Ellen Meiksins Wood, in her excellent book *Peasant Citizen and Slave: The Foundations of Athenian Democracy* (London: Verso, 1988) argues that the domination of agriculture by free peasants limited the growth and influence of slavery.

It was also stated by many that the position of women in Athens during the democracy was very bad. Naturally in these days, they did not have the vote. But for many centuries we were taught that the women of the Greek Democracy were little better than bearers of children and housekeepers for their husbands. Yet some modern writers, on closer examination of the evidence, have challenged the old view, and we believe that before very long, the world will have a more balanced view of how women lived in the Greek Democracy.

THE FOUNDERS OF WESTERN CULTURE

Now if the ancient Greeks had done little beside invent and practice this unique form of human equality in government, they would have done enough to be remembered. The astonishing thing is that they laid the intellectual foundation of Western Europe. Today when we speak about philosophy, logic, and dialect; when we speak of politics, democracy, oligarchy, constitution, and law; when we speak of oratory, rhetoric, ethics; when we speak of drama, tragedy, and comedy; when we speak of history; when we speak of sculpture and architecture; in all these things we use the terms and build on the foundations that were discovered and developed by the Greeks.

CORRESPONDENCE is not sure about science, but in every other sphere of human endeavor, whatever the methods, routines, procedures, etc. that are used by people in intellectual and political association with each other, these were discovered, invented, classified, and analyzed by the people of ancient Greece.

They not only invented or discovered these things. The men who invented and discovered and developed them – sculpture, politics, philosophy, art and literature, medicine, mathematics, etc. – these men are still to this day unsurpassed as practitioners of the things that they invented or discovered. If you were writing a history of modern civilization, you might find it necessary to bring in perhaps half a dozen Americans. Let us be liberal. A dozen. You will be equally in difficulty to find a dozen Englishmen. But in any such history of Western Civilization, you would have to mention some 60 or 80 Greeks.

Here are some of the names. Epic poetry – Homer. Dramatic poetry – Aeschylus, Sophocles and Euripedes. Comedy – Aristophanes. Lyric poetry – Pindar and Sappho. Statesmen – Solon, Themistocles and

Pericles. Sculpture – The Master of Olympia and Phidias. Oratory – Demosthenes. History – Thucyclides and Herodotus. Philosophy – Socrates, Aristotle and Plato. Science and mathematics – Pythagoras and Archimedes. Medicine – Hippocrates.

These are only some of the best known names. And the fact which should never be forgotten and which indeed we should make the foundation of all our thinking on Greece is that by far the greatest number of them lived, and their finest work was done, in the days when the Greek Democracy flourished.

MODERN COMPARISON

This is the greatest lesson of the Athenian democracy for us today. It was in the days when every citizen could and did govern equally with any other citizen, when in other words, equality was carried to its extreme, that the city produced the most varied, comprehensive and brilliant body of geniuses that the world has ever known. The United States today has a population of 155 million people. In other words, 1500 times the population of Athens. In economic wealth, any two-by-four modern city of 20,000 people probably contains a hundred times or more of the economic resources of a city like Athens in its greatest days. Furthermore, for a great part of its existence, the total citizen population of Athens could be contained in Ebbets Field or at any of a dozen football grounds in England. This will give you some faint idea of the incredible achievements not of ancient Greece in general, but of Greek Democracy. For it was the democracy of Greece that created these world-historical achievements and they could not have been created without the democracy.

Greece did not only produce great artists, philosophers and statesmen at a time when their work laid the foundation of what we know as civilization. The Greeks fought and won some of the greatest battles that were ever fought in defense of Western Civilization. At the battles of Marathon, Plataea and Salamis, a few thousand Greeks, with the Athenian democrats at their head, defended the beginnings of democracy, freedom of association, etc., against the hundreds of thousands of soldiers of the Oriental despotic monarchy of Persia. In those battles in the 5th Century, Oriental barbarism, which aimed at the destruction of the Greeks, was defeated and hurled back by the

Greeks fighting against odds at times of over 20 to 1. The Oriental despots knew very well what they were doing. They came determined to crush the free and independent states of Greece. Never before and never since was so much owed by so many to so few, and as the years go by the consciousness of that debt can only increase.

ATHENIAN DEMOCRAT – WHAT KIND OF MAN?

This has always been an important question but at the stage of society that we have reached, it is the fundamental question: What kind of a man was this Greek democrat? Karl Marx has stated that the future type of man, the man of a socialist society, will be a "fully developed individual, fit for a variety of labors, ready to face any change of production, and to whom the different social functions he performs are but so many modes of giving free scope to his own natural and acquired powers."

Here is how Pericles, one of the greatest statesmen of the Greek Democracy, described the ordinary Greek citizen:

> Taking everything together then, I declare that our city is an education to Greece, and I declare that in my opinion each single one of our citizens, in all the manifold aspects of life is able to show himself the rightful lord and owner of his own person, and do this, moreover, with exceptional grace and exceptional versatility.

Marx and all the men who have written of a society of democracy and equality had to place it in the future. For our Greek, this conception of the citizen was not an aspiration. It was a fact. The statement occurs in perhaps the greatest of all the Greek statements on democracy, the speech of Pericles on the occasion of a funeral of Athenians who had died in war.

The Greek democrat achieved this extraordinary force and versatility because he had two great advantages over the modern democrat. The first was that in the best days of the democracy, he did not understand individualism as we know it. For him an individual was unthinkable except in the city-state. The city-state of democracy was unthinkable except as a collection of free individuals. He could not see himself or other people as individuals in opposition to the city-state. That came later when the democracy declined. It was this perfect balance, instinctive and unconscious, between the individual and the city-state which gave him the enormous force and the enormous freedom of his personality.

Pericles shows us that freedom, the freedom to do and think as you please, not only in politics but in private life, was the very life-blood of the Greeks. In that same speech, he says:

> And, just as our political life is free and open, so is our day-to-day life in our relations with each other; We do not get into a state with our next-door neighbor if he enjoys himself in his own way, nor do we give him the kind of black looks which, though they do no real harm, still do hurt people's feelings. We are free and tolerant in our private lives; but in public affairs we keep to the law. This is because it commands our deep respect.
>
> We give our obedience to those whom we put in positions of authority, and we obey the laws themselves, especially those which are for the protection of the oppressed, and those unwritten laws which it is an acknowledged shame to break.

HUMAN "GODS"

Those simple words need hard thinking for us to begin to understand them today. The United States is notorious among modern nations for the brutality with which majorities, in large things as in small, terrorize and bully minorities which do not conform; in Great Britain, the conception of "good form" and "what is not done" exercises a less blatant but equally pervasive influence. The Greek democrat would have considered such attitudes as suitable only for barbarians. One reason why the Greeks so hated the Persians was that a Persian had to bow down and humble himself before the Persian King – the Greek called this "a prostration" and this too he thought was only fit for barbarians. Instead, in the midst of a terrible war, he went to the theatre (which was a state-theatre) and applauded a bitterly anti-war play by Aristophanes, and on another occasion, when the ruler of Athens, accompanied by foreign dignitaries, attended the theatre in his official capacity, Aristophanes ridiculed him so mercilessly in the play that he sued the dramatist – and lost the case.

Another great advantage of the Greek democrat was that he had a religion. The Greek religion may seem absurd to us today, but any serious study of it will show that it was as great an example of their genius as their other achievements. Religion is that total conception of the universe and man's place in it without which a man or a body of men are like people wandering in the wilderness. And the religious ideas of a people are usually a reflection and development of their responses to the society in which they live. Modern man does not know what to think of the chaotic world in which he lives and that is why he has no religion.

So simple and easy to grasp in all its relations was the city-state that the total conception with which the Greeks conceived of the universe as a whole and man's relation to it was extremely simple and, despite the fact that it was crammed with absurdities, was extremely rational. The Greek gods were essentially human beings of a superior kind. The Greeks placed them on top of a mountain (Olympus) and allowed them their superiority up there. But if any citizen looked as if he was becoming too powerful and might establish himself like a god in Athens, the Athenian Democracy handled him very easily. They held a form of referendum on him and if citizens voted against him, he was forthwith banished for ten years, though when he returned, he could get back his property. Gods were strictly for Olympus.

Around all religions there is great mystery and psychological and traditional associations which are extremely difficult to unravel. But, although the Greek no doubt recognized these mysteries, his relation to them was never such as to overwhelm him.

Thus in his relation to the state, and in his relation to matters beyond those which he could himself handle, he understood what his position was and the position of his fellow men in a manner far beyond that of all other peoples who have succeeded him.

WORKING POLITICS

In strict politics the great strength of the system was that the masses of the people were paid for the political work that they did. Politics, therefore, was not the activity of your spare time, nor the activity of experts paid specially to do it. And there is no question that in the socialist society the politics, for example, of the workers' organizations and the politics of the state will be looked upon as the Greeks looked upon it, a necessary and important part of work, a part of the working day. A simple change like that would revolutionize contemporary politics overnight.

The great weakness of the system was that, as time went on, the proletariat did little except politics. The modern community lives at the expense of the proletariat. The proletariat in Greece and still more in Rome lived at the expense of the community. In the end, this was a contributory part of the decline of the system. But the system lasted nearly 200 years. The Empires of France and Britain have not lasted very much longer. And America's role as a leader of world civilization is mortally challenged even before it has well begun.

THE GREEKS WERE A SOPHISTICATED PEOPLE

It is obvious that we can give here no more than a general account of Greek Democracy. There are great gaps in our knowledge of many aspects of Greek life; and even the facts that scholars have patiently and carefully verified during centuries can be, and are, very variously interpreted. There is room for differences of opinion, and Greek Democracy has always had and still has many enemies. But the position we take here is based not only on the soundest authorities, but on something far more important, our own belief in the creative power of freedom and the capacity of the ordinary man to govern. Unless you share that belief of the ancient Greeks, you cannot understand the civilization they built.

History is a living thing. It is not a body of facts. We today who are faced with the inability of representative government and parliamentary democracy to handle effectively the urgent problems of the day, we can study and understand Greek Democracy in a way that was impossible for a man who lived in 1900, when representative government and parliamentary democracy seemed securely established for all time.

Take this question of election by lot and rotation so that all could take their turn to govern. The Greeks, or to be more strict, the Athenians (although many other cities followed Athens), knew very well that it was necessary to elect specially qualified men for certain posts. The commanders of the army and of the fleet were specially selected, and they were selected for their military knowledge and capacity. And yet that by itself can be easily misunderstood. The essence of the matter is that the generals were so surrounded by the general democratic practices of the Greeks, the ordinary Greek was so vigilant against what he called "tyranny," that it was impossible for generals to use their positions as they might have been able to do in an ordinary bureaucratic or representative form of government.

PERICLES CRIES

So it was that the Greeks, highly sophisticated in the practice of democracy, did not, for example, constantly change the men who were appointed as generals. Pericles ruled Athens as general in command for some 30 years. But although he ruled, he was no dictator. He was constantly re-elected. On one occasion, he was tried before the courts but won a victory. On another occasion, Aspasia, the woman with whom he lived, was brought before the court by his enemies. Pericles defended her himself. He was a man famous for his gravity of deportment, but on this occasion, Aspasia was so hard pressed that he broke down and cried. The jury was so astonished at seeing this, that it played an important role in the acquittal of Aspasia. Can you imagine this happening to a modern ruler? Whether democratic or otherwise?

The Greek populace elected Pericles year after year because they knew that he was honest and capable. But he knew and they knew that if they were not satisfied with him, they were going to throw him out. That was the temper of the Greek Democracy in its best days.

This democracy was not established overnight. The early Greek cities were not governed in this way. The landed aristocracy dominated the economy and held all the important positions of government. For example, rich and powerful noblemen, for centuries, controlled a body known as the Areopagus and the Areopagus held all the powers which later were transferred to the council. The magistrates in the courts were a similar body of aristocrats who functioned from above with enormous powers such as modern magistrates and modern judges have. The Greek Democracy had had experience of expert and bureaucratic government.

It was not that the Greeks had such simple problems that they could work out simple solutions or types of solutions which are impossible in our more complicated civilizations. That is the great argument which comes very glibly to the lips of modern enemies of direct democracy and even of some learned Greek scholars. It is false to the core. And the proof is that the greatest intellectuals of the day, Socrates, Plato, Aristotle and others (men of genius such as the world has rarely seen), were all bitterly opposed to the democracy. To them, this government by the common people was wrong in principle and they criticized it constantly. More than that, Plato spent the greater part of his long life discussing and devising and publishing ways and means of creating forms of society, government and lay which would be superior to the Greek Democracy. And yet, Plato owed everything to the democracy.

Plato could think and discuss and publish freely solely because he lived in a democracy. We should remember too that the very ideas of what could constitute the perfect society he was always seeking, came to him and could come to him only because the democracy in Greece was itself constantly seeking to develop practically the best possible society. It is true that Plato and his circle developed theories and ideas about government and society which have been of permanent value to all who have worked theoretically at the problems of society ever since. Their work has become part of the common heritage of Western Civilization.

But we make a colossal mistake if we believe that all this is past history. For Plato's best known book, *The Republic*, is his description of an ideal society to replace the democracy, and it is a perfect example of a totalitarian state, governed by an elite. And what is worse, Plato started and brilliantly expounded a practice which has lasted to this day among intellectuals – a constant speculation about different and possible methods of government, all based on a refusal to accept the fact that the common man can actually govern. It must be said for Plato that, in the end, he came to the conclusion that the radical democracy was the best type of government for Athens. Many intellectuals today do not do as well. They not only support but they join bureaucratic and even sometimes totalitarian forms of government.

The intellectuals who through the centuries preoccupied themselves with Plato and his speculations undoubtedly had a certain justification for so doing. Today there is none. What all should study first is the way in which the Greeks translated into active concrete life their conception of human equality. The Greeks did not arrive at their democracy by reading the books of philosophers. The common people won it only after generations of struggle.

HOW THE DEMOCRACY WAS WON

It would seem that somewhere between 650 and 600 B.C., the first great stage in the development of Greek Democracy was reached when the laws were written down. The people fought very hard that the law should be written so that everyone should know what it was by which he was governed.

But this was not accidental. As always, what changed the political situation in Greece were changes in the social structure. Commerce and (to a degree more than most people at one time believed) industry; the use of money, played great roles in breaking down aristocratic distinctions, and over the years, there was a great social levelling, social equality, due to the growth of merchant and trading classes, to the increase of the artisan class, of workmen in small factories, and sailors on the ships. With these changes in Greek society, the merchants made a bid for power in the manner that we have seen so often in recent centuries in European history and also in the history of Oriental countries. Solon was the statesman who first established a more or less democratic constitution and, for that reason, his name is to this day famous as a man of political wisdom. We see his name in the headlines of newspapers, written by men who we can be pretty sure have little sympathy with what Solon did. But the fact that his name has lasted all these centuries as a symbol of political wisdom is significant of the immense change in human society which he inaugurated. A few years before the end of the 6th Century B.C., we have the real beginning of democracy in the constitution of Solon.

SOLON'S CONSTITUTION

The citizens of the city-state were not only those who lived in the city, but the peasants who lived around. Solon was supported by the merchants and the urban classes, and also by the peasants. The growth of a money economy and of trade and industry, as usual, had loaded the peasants with debt and Solon cancelled the burden of debt on them. So that in a manner that we can well understand, the growth of industry and trade, and the dislocation of the old peasant economy provided the forces for the establishment of Solon's great constitution. It was the result of a great social upheaval.

To give you some idea of the state of the surrounding world when Solon was introducing his constitution, we may note that 30 years after Solon's constitution, we have the death of Nebuchadnezzar, the king in the Bible who was concerned in that peculiar business of Shadrack, Meshak and Abednego. And this is the answer to all who sneer about the greatness of Greek Democracy. You only have to look at what the rest of the world around them was doing and thinking.

But although Solon's constitution was a great and historic beginning, the democracy that he inaugurated was far removed from the radical democracy, the direct democracy of later years. For at least a century after Solon, the highest positions of the state could only be filled by men who had a qualification of property and this property qualification was usually associated with men of noble birth. The constitution in other words, was somewhat similar to the British constitution in the 18th Century. The real relation of forces can be seen best perhaps in the army. In cities like Athens, the whole able-bodied population was called upon to fight its wars. Political power, when it passed from the aristocracy, remained for some decades in the hands of those who were able to supply themselves with armor and horses.

POWER OF ROWERS

About 90 years after Solon, there was another great revolution in Athens. It was led by a radical noble, Cleisthenes by name. Cleisthenes instituted a genuinely middle class democracy. As in Western European history, the first stage in democracy is often the constitution. Then later comes the extension of the constitution to the middle classes and the lower middle classes. That was what took place in Greece.

The great masses of the people, however, the rank and file, were excluded from the full enjoyment of democratic rights. The ordinary citizen, the ordinary working man, the ordinary artisan, did not have any of the privileges that he was to have later. The way he gained them is extremely instructive.

The development of commerce gradually transformed Athens first into a commercial city, and then into a city which did a great trade in the Mediterranean and the other lands around it. But a few years after the establishment of this middle class democracy by Cleisthenes, we have the period of the great Persian invasion. In 490 B.C., we have the battle of Marathon, in 480, the battle of Salamis, and in 479, the battle of Plataea, in which the whole population fought. Much of this war was fought at sea. Thus, commercially and militarily, Athens became a naval power. But the ships in those days were propelled by the men who rowed them. Thus the rowers in the fleet became a great social force. The Greeks always said that it was the growth of democracy which had inspired the magnificent defense of Greece against Persia. But after that victory was won, the rowers in the fleet became the spearhead of the democracy and they were the ones who forced democracy to its ultimate limits.

PROLETARIANS OF PIRAEUS

The port of Athens was, as it is to this day, the Piraeus. There, for the most part, lived the sailors of the merchant fleet and the navy, and a number of foreigners, as takes place in every great naval port. The leaders in the popular assembly were sometimes radical noblemen and later were often ordinary artisans. But the proletarians of the Piraeus were the driving force and they were the most radical of the democrats.

The struggle was continuous. The battle of Plataea took place in 479 B.C. A quarter of a century later, another revolution took place and power was transferred definitely from the nobles who still retained some of it, to the radical democracy. Pericles, an aristocrat by birth, was one of the leaders of this revolution. Five years after, the lowest classes in the city gained the power of being elected or chosen for the Archonship, a very high post. It was Pericles who began to pay the people for doing political work. From 458, the radical democracy continued until it finally collapsed in 338 B.C.

CLASS STRUGGLE

The struggle was continuous. The old aristocratic class and some of the wealthy people made attempts to destroy the democratic constitution and institute the rule of the privileged. They had temporary success but were ultimately defeated every time. In the end, the democracy was defeated by a foreign enemy and not from inside. One notable feature of Athenian democracy was that, despite the complete power of the popular assembly, it never attempted to carry out any socialistic doctrines. The democrats taxed the rich heavily and kept them in order, but they seemed to have understood instinctively that their economy, chiefly of peasants and artisans, was unsuitable as the economic basis for a socialized society. They were not idealists or theorizers or experimenters, but somber, responsible people who have never been surpassed at the practical business of government.

How shall we end this modest attempt to bring before modern workers the great democrats of Athens? Perhaps by reminding the modern world of the fact that great as were their gifts, the greatest gift they had was their passion for democracy. They fought the Persians, but they fought the internal enemy at home with equal, if not greater determination. Once, when they were engaged in a foreign war, the anti-democrats tried to establish a government of the privileged. The Athenian democrats defeated both enemies, the enemy abroad and the enemy at home. And after the double victory, the popular assembly decreed as follows:

> **ATHENIAN OATH**
> If any man subvert the democracy of Athens, or hold any magistracy after the democracy has been subverted, he shall be an enemy of the Athenians. Let him be put to death with impunity, and let his property be confiscated in the public, with the reservation of a tithe to Athena. Let the man who has killed him, and the accomplice privy to the act, be accounted holy and of good religious odor. Let all Athenians swear an oath under the sacrifice of full-grown victims in their respective tribes and demes, to kill him. Let the oath be as follows: 'I will kill with my own hand, if I am able, any man who shall subvert the democracy at Athens, or who shaft hold any office in the future after the democracy has been subverted, or shall rise in arms for the purpose of making himself a despot, or shall help the despot to establish himself. And if any one else shall kill him, I will account the slayer to be holy as respects both gods and demons, as having slain an enemy of the Athenians. And I engage, by word, by deed, and by vote, to sell his property and make over one half of the proceeds to the slayer,

> without withholding anything. If any man shall perish in slaying or in trying to slay the despot, I will be kind both to him and to his children, as to Hannodius and Aristogeiton and their descendants. And I hereby dissolve and release all oaths which have been sworn hostile to the Athenian people, either at Athens, or at the camp (at Samos) or elsewhere.' Let all Athenians swear this as the regular oath immediately before the festival of the Dionysia, with sacrifice and full-grown victims; invoking upon him who keeps it good things in abundance, but upon him who breaks it destruction for himself as well as for his family."

That was the spirit of the men who created and defended the great democracy of Athens. Let all true believers in democracy and equality today strengthen ourselves by studying what they did and how they did it.